# LET'S DON'T PAVE THE COW PATHS

## Lessons in Disruptive Leadership

John Covington

Tate Publishing, LLC
www.tatepublishing.com

# Dedication

I would like to dedicate this book
to my wonderful wife and partner, Linda,
and our daughter, Leigh.

# Table of Contents

# Foreword

*Do we really need another book on leadership? Haven't all the leadership theories been thoroughly discussed? What could another book possibly possess that would make it worth the investment of our time?*

*I have known John Covington well for many years. I first met him in his role as a business consultant. I have watched his business grow significantly through the years. He has attracted some very talented individuals, and together they built a great company. Obviously, John has demonstrated that elusive ability to lead, but I think there is more.*

*Though John is an accomplished businessperson, now known worldwide, what makes John special is that at his core he is a genuinely fine and caring human being. In addition, he has been blessed with an engaging sense of humor and a unique ability to communicate the complex in very simple terms.*

*When all of this is put together, we're able to answer the questions above. Yes, we need another book on leadership. And why is that? Because this book delivers. John communicates leadership truths that can help us all in an engaging way that makes the reading fun.*

*Time to get started. Now, John, just what is a cow path?*

*John Covington*

*Charles E."Gus" Whalen, Jr.*
*Chairman, Edward K. Warren Foundation*
*Gainesville, Georgia USA*
*June 4, 2005*

# PREFACE

Many business books I see are pretty dry. Worse than that, there often seems to be an underlying assumption that the business arena is completely different and divorced from every other area of life. Some of these authors would have you believe that all the wisdom and experience you've accumulated from being a parent, a pet owner, a shopper, a spouse, a frequent flyer and an oft-times observer of human behavior doesn't count at work. Somehow the rules are different there.

I beg to differ.

As a management consultant to many companies and a few not-for-profit organizations, I am struck by the similarities between work systems and all the other systems we are part of and know about. The world in which my old dog, Henry, must be neutered is the same world in which you may have to decide to lay off 15 percent of your employees. The world in which my teenage daughter requires 27 beauty products to take a shower is the same world in which you have 143 unread e-mail messages on your computer right now.

The system you work in is as dynamic as the system that is your family. It's as subject to natural law as the black snake that lived in a plant I once worked in, who was eaten by a new snake we introduced into his living quarters. And your workplace is as fraught with personal quirks and peculiarities as any system on earth. At least as fraught.

So it's always seemed to me that business leaders could learn—and maybe learn best—by analogies from other parts of life. If the concepts of some new management methodology or all-encompassing theories seem overly abstract, they can sometimes be sharply illuminated by a down-to-earth story. If the principle seems strange and hard to pin down, a parable about treating a dog's dry skin condition or dancing the conga might make it crystal clear.

I've been testing this proposition with Chesapeake Consulting clients for nearly twenty years now. Four times a year, we send them a newsletter which consists mostly of stories about the recent scrapes and strange adventures of my colleagues, our clients, and my household. Lots of people tell me this is the only newsletter they read. A gratifying number of them have fussed when we dropped them from the mailing list. And quite a few have suggested that I corral these stories into a book.

Like the world you live and work in, these stories are all about change. What do you change from? What do you change to? How do you make change happen? I would say that this book is a series of lessons in disruptive leadership.

Some of the essay writers whose work I've enjoyed most are Art Buchwald, Lewis Grizzard, and now, Dave Barry. But the business world doesn't seem to be blessed with many writers who are both wise and funny.

If you can't find the humor in things, then work, leadership, and life all become harder than they need to be. So I hope you'll find a few laughs in these pages. I hope you'll learn some things that will make all the turbulence you're dealing with easier and more fun to negotiate.

John Covington
April, 2005

# SOMETIMES YOU
## NEED A LITTLE
### COW POOP

Before I went into consulting, I had a real job. I used to "fix" and then manage plants. In the mid-1980s our family moved from East Tennessee to Baltimore, where I had been hired to manage a large paint plant.

The first week on the job was something of an adjustment period. The plant apparently had been taken over by aliens who wore ponytails. (This was before the days when boy lawyers began sporting ponytails.) These guys seemed to consider making paint a sidebar to drinking beer in the shop, mugging the security guards, pouring product on the floor, and a variety of other activities that were not in alignment with generally accepted manufacturing methods. One of the receiving operators tried to fly, by flapping his arms while diving off a tank car. He had been hanging with the guys in the red sweatsuits, who I later found out were the plant drug dealers.

At the end of that first week, I climbed on my white horse, headed to my safe suburban haven, and scanned the local phone book. "What are you doing?"

my lovely wife Linda asked. "I'm checking the address of the Baltimore Zoo," I told her. "I think I took a wrong turn."

To my dismay, I was at the correct location. I rued the day that I had made the foolhardy decision to leave the peaceful mountains of Tennessee. "Not to worry," Linda said. "You will change the culture of that plant. That's what you always do. The people who don't fit in with the new deal will be driven crazy. They'll either quit or fly off tankers. You just need to remember to take your cow poop to work for the initial phases of the transition."

Linda is familiar with the pattern. We start changing the culture by cleaning the place up. We put in a safety program that actually works, and through that, people begin to learn how to win. Then we make sure that everyone knows that the plant is supposed to produce paint that people would actually want to buy—a revolutionary concept. We also put in some new rules like . . . "It would be nice if you would come to work." These new rules take care of the drug dealers, who generally take exception at getting up at 5:00 a.m. on a consistent basis and putting in eight hours of making paint. After about ten months, this process usually starts to show some results.

Yet occasionally you have to use a little cow poop to turn around an operation. The logistics system I introduced at the Baltimore plant was based on Theory of Constraints concepts. If I was running the world, all manufacturing plants would incorporate the Theory of Constraints (TOC) principles, all business people would learn these concepts, and everybody would understand how constraints operate in all areas of their lives.

Since I firmly believe that TOC concepts are essential to successful organizational change, and since the phrase is going to keep turning up in anecdotes throughout this book, I'm going to digress for a minute here for an over-simplified summary of this theory. Here goes:

There is a limit to how much any system can produce. What that limit is will be determined by the weakest link, sometimes known as the bottleneck, sometimes called the most constrained resource. When you want to produce more, the Theory of Constraints tells us, the bottleneck becomes the focus of attention. First, you have to identify it (and believe me it is not always obvious). Then you use the constraint as the pacesetter to schedule the flow of work. Then you have to get all the other resources, especially the people, to change the way they work so as to get more through the bottleneck. Sometimes you might deliberately change what and where you want the most constrained resource to be.

At the paint plant, the constraint was the dispersing of pigment into the solvent, or what is called the grinding operation. There was a market for all the paint we could produce, and that grinding operation was limiting our output. It was the leverage point for the whole system.

**15**

So as soon I got to work in the morning, I would mosey on out to the constraint and see how things were going. Early on, the grinding operation was having a hard time staying on schedule because the necessary raw materials weren't on hand.

I went to Rick, the purchasing agent. "Production planning messed up the schedule, and if that ain't it, then the manufacturing guy must be fouled up," Rick said in a cooperative tone.

I suggested that Rick and I have a meeting with the scheduling and manufacturing folks. This was not in Rick's plan. Rick had planned for me to run back and forth among all of these different departments for three years or until I finally got tired, at which point I would either be promoted or fired. The first meeting was awful because Rick, the scheduler Bob, and the production guy Herman nearly came to blows.

I calmly pulled out my eight-pound sack of cow poop. "Gentlemen, here is what we are going to do," I said. "We are going to move your offices to the constraint location, and at each hour, you are to check to see if the constraint is on schedule. If it is not, each of you is to consume one tablespoon of cow poop."

The three men got very quiet. Then panic set in, as they realized that I was crazy and that this was not a joke.

Rick was the first to speak up. "I don't like cow poop, and besides, why should I do anything you say? You won't be here all that long anyway."

"Because if you do not do what I say, you will not be here to see me leave, you bozo," I calmly explained.

I think my fallback management style in those days was a bit on the primitive side.

Pretty soon the constraint was on schedule. The output of the plant increased by 25 percent with no additional capital expenditure, and nobody had to acquire a taste for cow poop.

By now *you* may think I am crazy. Not so. I may have just been ahead of my time. It must have been obvious to me that something very fundamental to that system was messed up. The basic dysfunction was in what we would now call the organizational culture. Today we also recognize that the essence of organizational culture is interconnected: *purpose, information, and relationships.*

We cannot expect the seeds of change and new knowledge to take root and grow if the culture—the soil—of the system is not good. That's why cow poop is so important. Let me explain:

Moving Rick, Herman, and Bob to the constraint location provided them with the *information* that they needed to stick with the schedule. They got to know each other better and communicated and cooperated more often, which improved their *relationships.*

My bag of cow poop gave them a common *purpose.* Up until then, Bob, Herman, and Rick were each looking out for themselves and focusing on their local objectives. In order to produce more paint, they were going to have to start acting in the best interest of the

**17**

whole system. This is still a tough point to get across and a tough transition to make in most organizations. Sometimes you need a little cow poop to get people to understand that they are now all responsible for the same results. The interdependence of systems is kind of an abstract concept, but the threat of eating cow poop is easy to understand. With Rick, Herman and Bob a little cow poop worked great.

If you create a culture that is focused on the majority of employees who want to be part of something bigger than themselves, then those who do not share this philosophy will leave on their own. That's good for them and good for your soil.

Then you can use the cow poop to grow some great tomatoes.

# HOW I LEARNED TO LOVE
## THE STRANGE ATTRACTOR

Linda and I were sitting in the little room in the hospital that's reserved for giving families bad news. Down the hall in one of the trauma rooms at Druid City Hospital in Tuscaloosa, Alabama, our only child, Leigh, was fighting for her life. Just the night before, my big concern had been whether Alabama was going to pull out a victory over Auburn, and my most immediate disappointment was that I was missing the live action. We had tickets to the game, but Leigh was sick with what looked like a bad case of bronchitis, so we elected to watch the game on TV.

It turned out to be fortunate that Linda and I were spending Thanksgiving in Tuscaloosa. What we thought was bronchitis was actually the symptoms of ketoacidosis, which is an extremely nasty way to find out that one is diabetic. The doctor later told us that he had never seen anyone survive who was in Leigh's condition.

It seems that a chain of small, specific, and separate events aligned to save Leigh's life:

Linda and I happened to be in town.

Acting on a gut feeling, I happened to go to her apartment on Sunday morning and found her nearly unconscious, in critical condition.

An emergency room nurse happened to notice something about the color of Leigh's legs that prompted her to get a doctor to look at her immediately.

A fast-acting trauma team accurately diagnosed the cause of her symptoms and began corrective action.

And of course, Leigh's strong constitution and a lot of fervent prayers also played a part.

Up until then, the plan was for Leigh to complete requirements for a university degree in May and launch her career. How quickly one discrete event can derail a strategic plan!

After the dust had settled and Leigh was hitting on about seven cylinders, she and I were having a philosophic discussion about the whole thing. I remarked how people who get the diagnosis that they are going to die before their time often ask, "Why me? Why do I have to die young?" My thought for Leigh was that maybe she should ask, "Why me? Why was I spared? What mission does God have in mind for me?"

Leigh thought about that for a second and said, "Dad, this sucks. Do you think God will mind if I just play dumb for a while longer?"

So much for philosophic discussions.

But you don't have to think hard or look far to find examples of the best-laid plans going astray. One mega-corporation buys another. Overnight, it's a whole new world for those companies, their employees, their suppliers, and probably their customers. An unwelcome medical diagnosis, an unplanned pregnancy, a freak accident, an unanticipated lay-off, a fire, a flood. . . . Stuff happens! Disruption and disorganization aren't just in the nature of things—they *are* the nature of things. Coming undone is a fundamental characteristic of both natural and manmade systems.

Much of what we see around us looks unpredictable and chaotic. To see order in apparent chaos requires a much larger perspective. From a distance and over time, the shape of the thing becomes clear. It may take a few more decades for Leigh to be able to know what came out of that life-threatening episode. However, history is full of examples of plans that fell apart, causing temporarily turbulent states that turned out to be the storm before the calm.

Take the United States, for example. At the birth of our nation, its purpose was clearly set forth in the Declaration of Independence and the Constitution. Over time, there was a drifting away from that strong, unifying vision. Local objectives became preeminent in some quarters, causing some states to secede from the larger organization. The terrible turbulence known as the Civil War was the result. But after that war had been fought, the North and South came together in a stronger union, with the commitment to life, liberty, and the pursuit of happiness reaffirmed at a deeper and higher level.

**21**

It's too soon to tell, but the terrorist attacks of September 11, 2001, may have had a similar effect. For several decades we have been drifting away from our united state, emphasizing our differences and our local agendas of ethnicity, race, gender, religion, and so on. The horribly disruptive events of that September day plowed through all the political correctness and local objectives to the deeper core of our common allegiance to the American dream of freedom and justice for all.

All kinds of systems have a tendency to loosen up over time. The tight alignment needed for optimum functioning gets messed up. Particles—or people—fly off in their own directions. Sometimes, in fact quite often, it takes painful disruption to reenergize a system, whether that is a family system, a political system, or a business system.

What pulls the system back into order is a force that scientists who study chaos call the *strange attractor.* It acts like a magnetic field to give things a specific shape. In human organizations, the strange attractor is mission and meaning, purpose, and principles.

What does this mean for you as a leader? Well, first of all, as you already know, lots of your plans are going to be disrupted by forces beyond your control, and those disruptions aren't necessarily bad.

Does this mean you should stop planning and just let nature take its course? I don't think so. Instead, you might focus your planning on building a strong, resilient system. A strong system is one in which *purpose, rela-*

*tionships,* and *information* are robust. You can proactively beef up these aspects of your organization, so that when disruption or disaster strikes, your company will be able to withstand the chaos and confusion and emerge even stronger. You can fortify the strange attractor.

You can also plan some disruption. Whatever stability has been achieved isn't going to last long anyway—that is the nature of things, remember? So why not be the one to throw the system into a transition state? If you're the one stirring things up, you can decide where to unleash the turmoil. You can concentrate the confusion on the leverage points in your system that are the keys to your survival and success.

Chaos theory explains why some apparently eccentric or erratic leaders achieve some of the best results. One of my mentors, for example, veered between two extremes. At one stage of running his organization he was a total control freak, which drove everybody crazy. At another stage, it seemed that he had almost no control over what happened, which drove everybody crazy. But as long as he stayed committed to the vision of the organization he had founded, and was perceived as being energized by those guiding principles, it really didn't matter how much control he exerted. The power of his vision—the strange attractor—pulled order out of chaos no matter how much turbulence his management style created. The people his vision had attracted to the organization were like highly charged molecules. When his control was lax, the "molecules" went with the flow.

When he tightened the reins, the walls of the organization ruptured like an over-pressurized tank. But after the disturbance, the molecules regrouped, in a similar configuration but with different boundaries. The purpose of the founder of the organization persisted—even when the founder himself was ousted during a period of turbulence and transition. The vision was clarified and confirmed in the process of disruption and reconfiguration.

If you look back on your organizational experience, I'm sure you'll find examples of this phenomenon. In a way, chaos theory just confirms common wisdom and ancient explanations of how things work. The Bible tells us that God created the universe out of chaos. Joe Diffie once had a country song that talked about chaos making sense. If it's in the Bible and country music, there must be some truth in it. And if you want to know more about how chaos theory applies to your organization, I highly recommend Margaret Wheatley's book, *Leadership and the New Science.* Dee Hock and Peter Senge have written perceptively and provocatively on this subject too.

The forces of chaos are already at work in your organization. It's not a matter of whether you buy into the theory of chaos. Chaos is there; it's the way of the world. The only variable is whether you recognize it and align your leadership to make the most of it.

In leaders, disruptiveness turns out to be a good quality, when the disruption created is thoughtful and intentional. Disrupting the status quo is a good way to make your organization fast, flexible, and strong enough to withstand the slings and arrows of outrageous fortune. Feeding and fortifying the strange attractor—the core vision and values of your organization—is a good way to ensure the long-term survival of that vision.

# DON'T LEAVE
# THE TOILET SEAT UP
## DURING NATIONAL NEUTER MONTH

As I write this, my good pal, Henry, is getting "neutered." That just sounds awful. Some of you guys may not want to read this chapter. Henry's dilemma comes from his not understanding the concept that time marches on, systems change, and an individual particle within that system may have to adapt.

Henry came to us as a Cairn Terrier pup, full of vim and vinegar. At the time, we also had a German Shepherd and a Siamese cat. Henry was low man on the totem pole; in fact, he was the only man on the totem pole as the other two were female. Henry has had a great dog life. He's had a ton of Naval Academy midshipmen to throw the ball for him, he's ridden around in all sorts of cars, and he's gone to lots of parties. One of his crowning moments was after his first confirmed mouse kill. The midshipmen dressed him in a Marine Corp scarf, and we got him a cigar, a bottle of beer, and a one-night stand with the poodle down the road. After seeing that reward, many of those midshipmen started hunting mice.

As time passed, the other two pets died and my wife, Linda, got Henry another Siamese cat, Dusty. A cat raised by a dog is neat for those of you who are not cat fans. In fact, this cat is so attached to the dog that when we board them the cat has to be in the same pen as Henry, or it will stop eating and try to kill itself.

Time continued to move ahead and Linda started to worry. "What are we going to do when Henry dies?" she fretted. "What will happen to poor Dusty?"

I guessed where this conversation was headed, but I figured I would at least put up a fight.

"Nothing will happen to the cat," I answered, hoping that would end the discussion.

"I recently read that animals mourn, "Linda said. "Dusty could die of grief."

Considering that Henry was doing just fine, this seemed to me to be unduly catastrophic reasoning. "We don't need another dog," I said firmly, hoping this would resolve the matter forever.

As you may have guessed, I lost that round and we had to get the cat a spare dog. Unbelievable! At least I won the gender battle, and we got a male spare dog.

As you can see, the system that Henry entered has radically changed, and he is now expected to be head of the Covington animal kingdom. This new role, along with a tad bit of aging, has put the damper on some of Henry's happy-go-lucky nature and occasionally he grumbles. Now Linda calls this grumbling "growling," but I think that's too harsh of a term. Sometimes Henry grumbles at the cat when she wants to steal a pig ear. Sometimes he grumbles at the spare dog after the spare dog bites him for the umpteenth time, and sometimes he grumbles at Linda, which is a real bad move, since he hardly ever grumbles at me. The grumbling at Linda normally takes place at bedtime when Henry and Linda fight over the same exact spot on the bed. Henry has been making some serious withdrawals from Linda's emotional bank account with this grumbling. Bad move on Henry's part.

One day Linda loaded the animal kingdom in the car to take them down for their shots. When she got back, she announced, "The vet thinks we should have Henry fixed."

(Don't you just love *that* term? Fixed, my hind parts!)

Henry gave out a big grumble.

"I bet it was a lady vet," I said.

"Well, yes, what's your point?" Linda replied.

"My point is she obviously dislikes all males and is trying to make Henry another victim. We should not let some crazy woman who is trying to make some sort of political statement 'fix' Henry. Henry is doing just fine being broken."

Henry's tail wagged profusely in agreement, but a few months later, there was an ominous development. I got the news when I called home from an out-of-town business trip.

"Henry wet in the house," Linda said grimly. "He peed on my plant and then growled at me when I fussed at him."

"Now hold on just a second, Honey," I replied. "Let's give Henry the benefit of the doubt. First of all, he wasn't growling; he was grumbling. At 70 years old in dog years, he's earned a certain amount of grumbling privileges. Second of all, I've been telling you that stupid plant is too big for the house. Heck, I'm sure Henry thinks it's a tree, and he naturally figured he was outside. The problem is not Henry; it's the tree."

I was trying to divert some of the flak from my little buddy, but I had a sinking feeling. Sure enough, Linda soon had the gang back at the vet.

"The vet says that the reason Henry peed on my plant is that his testosterone level is too high, and he needs to be fixed," she reported. "February is National Neuter Month, and we can have it done for half price."

"What! National Neuter Month? Whoever heard of such a thing? I bet you went to that same male-hating quacko. February is Black History Month. It's President's Day. It's Valentine's Day. Surely they would not have National Neuter Month so close to Valentine's Day. That's criminal! What's this country coming to?"

By now Henry and the spare dog were hiding under the bed in the guestroom, and the neutered cat was laughing. Linda had a determined look on her face. I sat there in stunned silence with my legs crossed.

The next day I called my long time friend and fellow Chesaperson, Ed Ligon, for advice. Surely he would have some words of wisdom.

"Ed, we have a crisis at our house," I said.

"What's the problem?"

"It's National Neuter Month, and Linda wants to get Henry fixed. Henry is pushing his luck. He's been grumbling at Linda and squirting on one of her stupid plants. I believe she is just looking for an excuse to have him fixed."

"Well, Nancy had me fixed, and it wasn't so bad," Ed replied in a high-pitched voice.

"What! I know Nancy, and she wouldn't do something like that. What would possess her to do such a thing?"

"I think it had something to do with not wanting any more kids," Ed said. "Also, I was marking my territory, and I left the toilet seat up."

"That's not funny, Ed! You've been no help at all. I've got to run."

"Oh, John."

"What!"

"One last thing. Don't leave the toilet seat up during National Neuter Month, or Linda will have you fixed too. He, he, he," he said in his high-pitched voice.

"A lot of help he was," I grumbled to myself. Things were starting to come apart at the seams. Then Stephanie, one of our administrative assistants who used to work for a nut company told me to call home. When

Linda answered the phone, she didn't waste any words.

"*Your* dog peed on my new quilt—the one made by the Amish ladies. He has an appointment on February 12 to be fixed, and that's that!"

And it was. Happy Valentine's Day, Henry.

Is there anything we, as business folks, can learn from my little buddy? Absolutely! Don't worry so much about marking your territory is one moral of the story. Limiting your grumbling is another.

Seriously, we often see "protection of turf" at our client companies. We have yet to have someone pee in the corner of the building to mark his or her territory, but we have heard a fair amount of grumbling and growling. Of course, a lot of this territory marking and grumbling has nothing to do with improved global performance, but it has to do with ego, politics, and the desire to control.

Every organization has its "Henrys"—folks who have been with the organization for a long time and have established their behaviors based on a certain set of paradigms. Much of my dog's behavior is programmed by instinct and would be pretty difficult to change. Our human systems can sometimes be programmed, but given that we have freedom of choice, we can always elect to change our programming. Old and young folks like Henry can and do change programming (assumptions) and learn to bark happily and wag their tails in new and changing environments. The duty of our organizations is to provide the calm and gentle disruptions and learning experiences to allow this to happen. Living with the limiting paradigms is never an option, and in the long run, it will be self-correcting—one way or the other.

The systems that we are part of are changing faster than ever. That hard shell that we can have around our departments—and perhaps ourselves—limits our ability to connect with other people and other departments. This makes it difficult for our systems to be flexible and successful when the environment is requiring rapid and different responses. Protective capacity is required for your system's stability and cannot be wasted on the inefficiencies caused by high internal silos with thick walls.

# WHAT TO DO
## WHEN THE SYSTEM
### IS DOWN

I believe my daughter Leigh is ahead of her time. She is trying to motivate her employees to consider using a systems approach to thinking. Wisely, she is starting by trying to get them to think at all. Leigh is a restaurant manager, and several months ago an enthusiastic employee came up and said, "Hey Leigh, give me something to do!"

"Why don't you grab a bucket and empty the water out of the coffee pot," Leigh replied.

As the young man went off to find a bucket, another employee said, "Leigh, the coffee pot is fed directly from our water line. He will never empty the coffee pot."

"Correct!" Leigh said. "Let's see how long it takes him to figure it out."

She was obviously trying to teach this young man the value of thinking before going off half-cocked. (See how nice dads are! Most folks would have assumed she was yanking this guy's chain.)

Although they don't have to be, computers are often a deterrent to common sense thinking. Not to say I told you so, but I predicted the end of the world was beginning when we abandoned slide rules. Now I am being proved correct. Folks just aren't thinking as well as they used to.

Here's a typical example. Just last week I was at a church meeting and I asked the question, "How much money was in the offering in January?"

"We couldn't determine this because the computer was down all month," our financial person said.

Thank heavens we have a forgiving Lord, as what blurted out of my mouth next was, "Er, we are not dealing with a Laplace transform here. Isn't this a simple addition problem where we add four weekly deposit slips?"

Take another recent example. We were talking with the president of a company about what was needed to move their company to the next step change in performance. They had been considering large software packages ranging from ERP systems to industry specific software. Someone in their organization suggested consulting Chesapeake, so we spent a day wandering around with them. The situation was that sales had increased at a pace much faster than manufacturing could increase capacity. Their business system was teetering on the brink of being unstable, but was not yet totally out of control.

At the end of the day, we suggested that instead of running out and buying a new computer system they should take a few other steps first, including:

1. Decide what business system they were dealing with.

2. Determine whether they wanted to lead with capacity or lead with demand.

3. Understand the processes for increasing capacity and increasing demand and how should they be synchronized.

4. Teach their folks to be able to recognize unstable systems and to make the necessary changes to gain stability. We emphasized that this knowledge and wisdom needs to be embedded *in people* not just in the rules of software.

5. Figure out and have a vision for how the company flows, including what information is required. Then, and only then, go find a software package that meets their needs.

In the meantime, get to work and start getting some of the improvement that comes from improved stability and thinking.

The point is to subordinate the software to the way you decide to do business, not the other way around. The president looked a tad taken back and replied, "That makes way too much sense," and we both had a laugh.

One more example of how computers have given so many of us permission to stop using our heads. Back when I had a real job, my head of purchasing, production, and inventory control came into my office all worried. His name was Bob and he worried a lot. Bob spent much of his day poring over computer reports, and he carried the then familiar green-and-white lined paper with the holes in it everywhere he went. This day was no exception. The computer had alerted him to some sort of imminent disaster, and he had come to warn me. To me, the problem appeared to be a relatively simple issue.

"Bob, does what you just said sound smart?" I asked him. He coughed a couple of times and seemed to be in shock. "Bob," I said, "throw that computer printout in that trash can and sit down. Now explain to me what in the heck you would do if you owned this joint, realizing that folks don't stop using our product just because your computer acts stupid on occasion."

After some additional dialogue, Bob came up with a good solution based on his common sense and intuition about the flow of material. I then explained to Bob that if he and his folks continued to rely on the computer system to do their thinking rather than as a tool to give specific information, then I was going to shut the system down. We would just do it by hand for awhile until we all knew what the heck we were doing. Although I had only been there about a year, Bob was already totally convinced that I was crazy, so he figured this was not an idle threat.

I would much rather have high-level decisions come from informed folks rather than those nice geeks who embedded the rules and programmed the software. Although they are all convinced that their software is the best, the vast majority has never led a horse to water, and they are unqualified to understand true systemic change. If they were, then there would not be so many failed software implementations. And believe me, there are a lot of failed and stalling software implementations.

The bible for many software companies is the book *Crossing the Chasm*. This book has convinced these companies that they must supply a "whole solution" and many have leaped to the decision that they must be the ones to supply this whole solution on their own. (After hearing about "whole solutions," my dentist now claims he can do heart surgery. If your dentist starts to unbutton your shirt, get up and get out of there.)

Deep-seated assumptions and prejudices lead to rules and policies that cause constraints where you don't want them. Only true knowledge transfer can blow these prejudices away. This is the role of leadership, not software. Buying a software package is not going to solve your business problems. There is a lot more to it than that.

I hesitate to write this, as I know I'm going to catch some flak, and I like to minimize my diet of flak, but I am frustrated at the number of smart people in institutions everywhere who sometimes act brain dead and assume no responsibility for taking proactive moves to make things better. Many feel that since they bought the software that all will be just fine, and they can sit on their hands. Meanwhile, it has been our experience that software companies do a relatively poor job of moving the implementation past the technical installation of software to the real operations level. The problems normally don't surface until a year or so after the initial euphoria of an implementation. By then, many of the players have moved on, leaving a mess behind.

Have you ever gotten the excuse "Our computer system is down, and I have forgotten how to think, so I cannot give you good service"? Not quite in those words, but I have.

I was talking with a computer company several weeks ago and asked the question, "Do you ever have to go back to an account that has stagnated and help them again?" Laughter filled the room. Then the follow-up question, "Will this impact your ability to bring on new business and grow your revenues?" No laughter this time. The issue is one for both the software companies and their customers.

So what's the point? The point is that if you are in the line organization of your company, then you need to know how your business works and occasionally check to make sure that common sense is sneaking into the system.

Think this it is not a problem? Well, don't you wish that 40 or so years ago some line leader had said, "Hey, propeller head! Do you think the world is going to end in 1999? If not, then you better change this darn code to count the year 2000."

Perhaps it is time for us to start thinking for a change.

# THE COMMON SENSE
# THERAPIST IS IN

Recently several of us Chesafolks were having lunch, and Liz Judy was bemoaning the fact that her massage therapist was going on a two-year sailing trip. We do not tease Liz about having two first names, as she is the one who handles our money, including payroll. Mess with Liz, and you are liable to find your direct deposit in cyberspace headed for Turkey. However, I only have so much self-control.

"Massage therapist?" I asked. "Are you kidding me? What in the heck is a massage therapist?"

Come to find out, there are all kinds of therapists. There are music therapists, dance therapists, dog therapists, sleep therapists, and of course, the good old kick-'em-in-the-teeth therapist therapists. It doesn't take much to get our gang going, so we were hooting it up about all these different kinds of therapists. Someone came up with the idea that if we called ourselves therapists instead of consultants that we could charge more money. I'm pretty sure that was Liz's idea. That led to another round of hooting, and someone said that we could be "common-sense therapists." We were already making plans for where we would put the couch.

We developed mental images of Lisa Scheinkopf and Ed Hill gently asking a client, "And just how did you feel after that mean old policy constraint caused you to miss all your shipments last month?" After that session, I was starting to worry that *we* needed a therapist.

So off we went to do an extensive market survey to see if the world of business needs some common-sense therapists. Our first stop was an airline where our own Bill Hodgdon fell asleep waiting for a flight. When Bill awoke from his nap, the waiting area was vacant except for him and the folks behind the desk.

Bill waltzed up to the counter and asked, "When does the flight for Cincinnati leave?"

"Sir, that flight left 30 minutes ago," the nice lady told him.

"What? Why didn't you wake me?"

"But you were asleep."

"Do you honestly think I came to the airport to sleep?" Bill asked her in his usual calm manner. We recorded the airlines as needing a common-sense therapist and Bill as needing a sleep therapist.

Our next stop was the APICS Theory of Constraints meeting in Phoenix. We didn't expect to see a lack of common sense, but we were pleasantly surprised to find a market there also. Lisa ran into some nice fellow who told her all about an internal constraint in his plant. This guy had learned the Theory of Constraints decision-making processes, and by gosh, he was going to apply them.

"Yes, Lisa," he told her. "I am going to go down there on the shop floor and help those folks do their trees in this analysis."

"Isn't this physical constraint so obvious that your five-year-old could find it?" Lisa asked in her customary tactful way.

"It is, but I need to do my current reality tree," he said.

"Current reality!" Lisa replied. "You need to get your head out of the clouds and come on over here and lay down on this couch. You need a common-sense therapist."

At this same conference, I attended an educational session on supply chains. We were all happily playing a game with jellybeans when the instructor said, ". . . and then we institutionalize the change with software." Three thoughts popped to mind:

Lots and lots of money.

Lots and lots of time.

Dilbert, Wally, Alice, and the pointy-haired boss "institutionalizing" me. This is the same crew that brought us the Y2K bug.

I thought, *Wow, if we can find people who actually believe they have to have software to institutionalize change, then we will have found a herd of folks who need a common-sense therapist.* Yahoo! We will be able to mint money, and Liz can buy the bank that holds our line of credit. All we have to do is find those companies that have spent

**45**

a bazillion dollars on some ERP or APS system, and we will have a target-rich environment.

Want to argue with this? One of the keynote speakers at this conference was Dr. Margaret Wheatley. She told us that in a recent study of Fortune 500 CEOs, these executives estimated that 75 percent of major improvement efforts (including software implementations) fail. Seventy-five percent! Folks, that is what they admitted to. As you know, the number is probably higher.

Why is this so? I don't know, but let's take a stab at it. One reason might be an over-reliance on technology. Another might be buffalo-herd mentality. Many of us in business are engineers, scientists, accountants, and others who may be more comfortable with technology than we are with people or "softer" issues in business. We want a technical answer to our improvement question. We are uncomfortable with the chaotic and dynamic nature of business systems. If a technology company comes to us with a snap-in solution (even if they're charging a bazillion dollars for it) and everyone else is jumping on that bandwagon, it lessens the emotional risk of making that purchase.

Perhaps a larger reason for project failure may be the premature or improper deployment of a tool. Information technology is usually not the first answer to your business problem; it is a tool. The combined leadership wisdom and knowledge of what tool to use and when to use it is the answer. There are numerous tools out there that you should be aware of and probably know how to use. They include statistical methods to improve quality, decision-making methodologies, and information technology.

If a tool is applied poorly or at the wrong time, the possibility of collateral damage can be high. The young man trying to introduce Theory of Constraints by using some of its processes to address an obvious problem is probably not going to do too much harm. It will just take longer than necessary to deal with the problem, and several of the operators in the plant will think he is weird. However, buying a new computer system too early can do damage for a decade. This has been a pet peeve of mine for nearly 20 years, and the problem has progressively gotten worse.

If you plan to embark on a supply chain project, information technology should be the last thing you invest in—not the first. Please note that I did *not* say, "Do not invest in technology." What I am saying is, determine what information your new system will require first. There are several reasons for this:

Whether it is an internal supply chain or one that involves suppliers and customers, you will more than likely redefine what you are calling a system. You certainly do not want to "institutionalize" anything prior to that (but that is actually what many companies are doing).

When you redefine your business system, you will probably run into some significant organizational issues.

**47**

If not, then you probably haven't done squat. This new system will require that people learn to work together and strive for a common purpose.

You can gain the vast majority of the financial benefit claimed by most software companies without purchasing the software. In many years of consulting, I have never seen a company prevented from getting significant improvement because their existing information system could not give them the required information. You can make a bazillion bucks *before* you purchase the software.

The above steps will probably take 6–24 months, depending on the size of your enterprise. Systems are held together by purpose, relationships, and yes, information. Your new business system will dictate what information you will need. At that point, you should consider purchasing an information system. By this time, you will be in the position to buy what you need versus being sold what they have. It should also cost you less money.

You will lessen your chance of being one of the 75 percent.

Information technology is part of any significant change, but it should be subordinate to what is required by a newly defined business system. This is not a trivial difference, and it has an impact on the cost benefit of the software package.

Perhaps we all need an extra dose of common sense. We need to improve upon that 75 percent failure rate. We need to be less reliant on computer systems and more reliant on our knowledge of natural systems and the people who help make up those systems.

# PRIDE AND PREJUDICE
## AND PARADIGM SHIFTS

It was in the early '70s. A young African-American woman was approaching a red light in Tuscaloosa, Alabama. At the same time, I was walking with several other young white males toward the light. We were coming from some sort of a science lab. As she came to the stoplight, the woman leaned over and locked her passenger door. We made eye contact, and I couldn't help but chuckle to myself, "It sure works both ways." The young woman had "prejudged" us because of our age, gender, and the color of our skin.

I was reminded of that little episode in the wake of the terrible terrorist attacks of September 11, 2001. I teach an adult Sunday school class, and the Sunday after the attack, one of our associate pastors left some reading matter that he hinted we should discuss in the class. It was material on how Christians and Muslims needed to get along and understand one another. I couldn't do it. I was in no mood to understand anything along those lines, much less teach it. I felt myself getting angry that he would even suggest such a thing. He could take his liberal pacifist views and stick them where the sun doesn't

**51**

shine. I have never viewed myself as a bigot, and I do not think others have either. However, maybe I am one. I know those Middle Eastern folks cheering in the streets and waving anti-American slogans are bigots.

One of the papers in the area listed 11 terrorist attacks on U.S. interest over the last 25 years. Timothy McVey committed one; radical Islamics committed the other ten. I suspect we have a lot of folks who are coming to grips with their "prejudging."

Prejudging is not all bad and is nothing more than our assumptions about certain things. These assumptions are learned, and in many cases, they protect us from harm. The African-American lady in Alabama took action on her prejudice in order to protect herself. Living in Alabama at that time, I can understand why she had these assumptions. As the offended party, I need to understand that. This lady was probably a very nice person, and if we got to know one another, I am guessing she would probably like me and would not lock her car door the next time she saw me coming. Getting to know one another would probably be more my responsibility than hers—if, of course, I wanted to help her understand that I was not someone to be feared. I have a choice; I can sulk because someone showed bias toward me, or I can work to eradicate the misconception that caused it. I probably cannot do both.

Many of these assumptions about life (prejudices) are in our subconscious, and we do not think about them. September 11 brought a whole lot to the surface and perhaps created more assumptions. Let's say that you and I are going to fly somewhere together. You are of Arab descent, Islamic, and not a U.S. citizen. I'm sorry, Pal; I am not going to be as comfortable as I would be if you were from China or Ohio. That may be an old prejudice that just surfaced, or it may be one that was just created. It probably doesn't matter how it got there; it is there. No political correctness is going to take that away. You and I both are going to have to live with it until a better day—a day when we know one another better.

They key word here is "we" deal with it. Normally, the onus is on the bigot to become a better person and not to have these biases. That really hasn't worked in the past, so why should we think it would work now? True knowledge transfer is about how we address erroneous assumptions or prejudices that are not grounded in fact. The President of the United States speaking from a Mosque began some valuable knowledge transfer for me. A man I respect was saying that all these Muslim folks are not bad, so I listened. Then several Muslim nations led by moderates aggressively supported our country and the principles of freedom—more knowledge for old John. The folks who run our local Subway sandwich shop are Middle Eastern Muslims. I stopped by there, and I found myself hoping that they were not experiencing negative feelings. They appear to be nice people; I would hate to see them hurt. I am closer to being able to teach that literature that our pastor gave me—not there yet, but closer than I was. Perhaps I will keep learning and will discover

**53**

my assumptions were and are erroneous. I hope so.

I hope so because I do not want to cause harm that is not just. For example, if you fire someone from your company you have harmed them. If you caught them in the act of stealing, harming them would be just. We walk a fine line each day.

So what can we learn about improvement and business? A lot, I think. None of the folks at Chesapeake have a degree in psychology. The majority of us are geekie engineering types. In doing what we do, however, we've had to learn some things about prejudice. A ten-dollar word for prejudice is "paradigm." We deal with that fancy type of prejudice all the time. Entire industries have paradigms. Many of these prejudices are so deep seated that it is difficult to introduce new ideas and technologies that would improve things.

Here's an example of what I mean. I entered the paint industry from the chemical process industry. I am probably "prejudiced," but it has always been my belief that the chemical process industry was a couple of leaps ahead of the rest of the planet with respect to technology and cool ways to do things. I think a lot of that expertise came from the fact that a mistake in chemical processing causes real bad things to happen fast. The first paint company I worked for did color matching by eye instead of using a color computer. Although the technology was there, most paint companies at that time did not use computers to match colors. This really is a no-brainer; the computer gives superior matches and can save huge additional cost in excess colorant. Eventually, the industry shifted over, and I doubt there are any companies that still use non-computer generated color matches. The deep-seated belief that color matching was an "art" probably delayed the acceptance of this technology for at least a decade. For a decade, the problem was not technical; it was mental.

Similarly, at one time many people in manufacturing companies felt that lots of inventory was a good thing. Believe it or not, that belief is still out there, even though we have had two decades of evidence that reducing inventory increases speed and predictability.

Nevertheless, there are many beacons of light and hope in industry. Chesapeake is fortunate to be associated with lots of companies that challenge deep-seated beliefs in order to improve. When they do this, they are doing the best they can to bring intervals of security, profitability, and stability to their stakeholders. Stanley Furniture is one such company. I have a soft spot in my heart for those folks, as they were one of our first large accounts. They are also pretty nice people. In the early '90s, we proposed some pretty radical changes in the way they flowed material through their business system. The new policies flew directly in the face of many well-established industry paradigms. Stanley overcame those prejudices and has been the leader in the industry with respect to quality and service.

Times have changed. Now Stanley is looking to make additional changes to reflect a changed world.

However, this time they will be challenging deep-seated paradigms from a position of strength and profitability. Victory and success sometimes can cloud our vision as much as adversity.

So what's the point? I guess the point is to realize that we all have those hidden assumptions, even those people who fuss at the rest of us for having them. Some of those assumptions are valid, and they serve to protect us. Some are erroneous, and they serve to hurt us and others. This holds true on any scale, whether individual, family, company, or global. Let's concern ourselves with the erroneous assumptions that cause damage. On a global scale, these assumptions are caused by ignorance, hopelessness, and poverty. I imagine some of that applies to how we address the problem on any scale. Perhaps the best we can do is to:

Constantly challenge and seek verification for what you believe to be true.

Remain open minded.

Never stop learning. Seek wisdom.

Look at environments outside your business for a better understanding of your business. All systems exhibit similar universal truths.

The events of September 11 have changed all of us. We are all back to getting things accomplished with a greater sense of resolve and with an appreciation of making the best of the time we have been granted in order to make a difference. We will make a bigger difference if we confront and conquer erroneous prejudices that rob us of our human potential.

# IDENTITY CRISIS
## IN THE CONVENT

It is 5:18 a.m., and I am writing this from the Congregation of Our Lady of the Retreat in the Cenacle, which is a convent. Go ahead and laugh. My wife, Linda, hasn't stopped chuckling since I told her. When our daughter was a teenager, I used to threaten her with, "If you don't shape up, I'm going to send you off to a Methodist nunnery!"

Now I don't know if such a thing exists, but can you imagine her reaction last night when her mother told her, "Leigh, your dad can't call you tonight, as he's locked up in a convent."

There are not a whole lot of things to do in a convent other than to pray and write. Let me assure George Ennis, our pastor in Severna Park, that I have been praying. One of my prayers is that a TV with ESPN will appear in my room by tonight so I can watch the Alabama—Vanderbilt game. I don't think that is going to be one of God's priorities, but I will probably survive.

Convents are interesting places and are a tad different from the hotels in which we generally stay during an assignment. I am in Room 504, which does not have a phone, TV, or bathroom. Fortunately, I am not much taller than one of the sisters, as the beds are short. Several of the taller fellows put their mattresses on the floor. We learned that we could thank Ezra Earl Jones, who is General Secretary of the Board of Discipleship of the United Methodist Church (UMC), for these accommodations. Although a visionary leader, Ezra Earl is cheap—er, frugal, that is. I'm certain he got a great deal on the rooms. Lisa Scheinkopf and I are here working with the UMC in a strategic planning session. Lisa is Jewish, so staying in a convent is even stranger for her. As Lisa says, "I am way outside my comfort zone."

The leadership of the UMC is as good as any we have run across. Lisa and I commented several times, "How would you like to start a company and have these folks as your leadership team?" The group consists of several bishops from across the country, and for lack of a better term, support functions out of their headquarters in Nashville. A bishop would be like a division president and God is the chairman of the board. In our strategic planning process, we start off spending some significant time learning about systems theory. Without an understanding of the chaotic nature of systems and the role leadership plays in such systems, it is difficult to do meaningful planning. The majority of this group has already been through some systems learning with Margaret Wheatley, and some have been through our six-day thinking process course. It is a group well armed for planning. Our job as facilitators was made much easier by their previous preparation and knowledge. We also found that they got a lot more value out of us, because we took them to a level of discussion that we don't get to with most clients.

As hard headed as I am, occasionally I learn something from assignments. Let me see if I can share what sunk in at the convent. During our explanation of how systems were held together by purpose, relationships, and information, Ezra Earl (the frugal visionary leader responsible for me missing the Alabama—Vanderbilt game) spoke up and told me I was nuts, and that it was not purpose but "identity" that needed to be stressed. I am just a simple-minded redneck and "purpose" works for me. I can go kick "purpose" or "mission" and make something happen. I'm thinking to myself, "Uh oh, here comes the fluff!" One of my fears about working with church folks is that they will not lower their heads and be disruptive enough, because they are so nice, and they tend to shy away from conflict.

The chance of disrupting a system appears to me much greater if one has a clearly stated purpose and the fuzzy term of "identity" seemed too weak to make a difference. I guess my fuzzy logic needs a little work. By the way, did you catch that? Good leaders are disruptive. If you ain't disruptive, you ain't leading, and being nice and being disruptive are not mutually exclusive. Living systems are not led; they are disrupted. Constraint management principles help us to focus the disruption so we can leverage our efforts.

*Ezra Earl, have you lost your mind? How are we going to rally around "identity?"* I thought. However, I had way too much tact and diplomacy to say. I now figured that I must be in the room with a bunch of quacko, liberal Democrats (including Lisa). Us right-winged, reactionary Republican quacks were seriously outnumbered. The thing that bothered me is that Ezra Earl had a good point that needed to be pondered. It concerns me when I almost agree with quacko, liberal Democrats.

Perhaps a condition a company would like to achieve is one in which there is a clear understanding of identity. People (or particles in physics) do not have identity without connection to others (relationships). The intensity of these relationships is critical, and common purpose helps determine the strength and intensity of the relationship. One of the core issues facing the UMC is that they perceive, in general, they do a poor job of spiritual formation, and this very well could affect their identity. What they mean by spiritual formation is that an individual Christian progresses through stages of Christian maturity. As this progress evolves, people gain a clearer picture of their identities with God and with others. Before I mess up and make God mad, let me switch to some other analogies right quick.

I did escape the convent and am now on a 757 en route to San Francisco. As a group of travelers on this plane, we already have a small identity, as we are all passengers on Flight 47 out of Baltimore, with a somewhat mundane, non-exciting purpose. Let's say this plane has to make an emergency landing, and we end up in the forest somewhere and have to hike to the nearest town. Now all of a sudden, the importance and excitement of purpose has been elevated, and there is much more intensity and clarity. What do you think that just did for the relationships? Of course, these relationships would now be more intense and focused. The group would have a heightened identity to the point that we might even have a reunion once every five years or so just to remember the experience. In fact, I bet that this particular group would probably be quite effective tackling a number of tasks.

I have noticed the same type of phenomenon both in facilities I have managed and in consulting assignments over the last decade. Verbalization of a clear-cut common purpose (and a way to measure performance) that is in alignment with the goal of the organization and not in conflict with the individual's value system goes a long way toward achieving improved performance and clarifying this mystical state of "identity." I wouldn't take this too lightly. Many organizations that may have started with clear-cut and easy-to-understand purposes have become lukewarm and dispassionate. Sometimes individual parts within the system have a difficult time connecting their actions with the overall system purpose. The danger here is that the system begins to lose identity—which might be the equivalent of low, personal self-esteem. That ain't good.

# OUT OF THE CANOE,
# INTO THE CHAOS

This chapter *was* going to address a romantic encounter of one of our clients and his wife in a canoe. I was going to use the encounter to illustrate the concepts of equilibrium and chaos theory and how they tie to organizational systems—important stuff for leaders to know. I thought this was a great way to address two critical areas of knowledge that you as leaders should understand: the new sciences and how to make whoopee in a canoe.

Then I sat down in the den and asked Linda if she wanted to hear my latest chapter. This is the girl of my dreams and the only one on the planet who ever laughed at my warped sense of humor. "Of course, I want to hear it," she said. Also in the den were Henry, our boy Cairn Terrier, and Dusty, our girl Siamese cat.

I get into the juicy part of the story, and Henry and I are in almost uncontrollable laughter. I could tell Henry was laughing because his tail was going in circles. Dogs do a lot of talking with their tails. It was really funny. After several minutes Henry and I realized that we were the only ones laughing. Linda was giving me one of those stares, and the cat's tail was fluffed up like a pine tree. Based on my limited knowledge of cats and wives, I believe that means they did not think the chapter was funny.

"What's wrong?" I asked.

"I think talking about sex in your book is inappropriate," Linda said.

"But I cleared this with ol' Jerry (not the client's real name)," I protested. By now the cat was hissing at me.

"Did you get ol' Jerry's wife to approve?" Linda asked in a frosty sort of way. "Do you know what I would do to you if *I* were Jerry's wife?"

Henry exited the den with his tail between his legs. The cat sat there laughing. Oh well, funny chapter quickly canceled.

So this chapter has nothing to do with canoes. It is about knowledge, your culture and some thoughts on what holds organizational culture together.

If you are in the role of a leader, you are supposed to change stuff for the better. According to many, the recipe for change that brings improvement is *knowledge, skill,* and *desire.* It's *not* going to change if you don't have those three. You might be saying, "Knowledge of what?" Let's explore that. Edward Deming, the father of the quality movement, listed four areas of knowledge required for organizations:

1. Variability

2. Psychology
3. Systems
4. Creative, strategic or systems thinking
We have added another:
5. Information Technology.

*Variability* is our Total Quality Management education, specifically what we know about process variation. *Psychology* is that part of our knowledge base that helps us deal better with folks, and it would cover the issues of self-directed work teams and why the same people perform differently under different leadership. Coach Bear Bryant used to say, "I can take my guys and whip ya, or I can take your guys and whip ya." This might be the category where one would put in shared vision, purpose, and meaning of the organization. *Systems* is the stuff Chesapeake Consulting does and would cover constraint management, throughput accounting, synchronous flow, finite scheduling, continuous flow, time-based management, reengineering, or whatever your favorite buzzword is for knowing what to do with business flow and how to do it faster for more profit. *Creative, strategic, or systems thinking* is an interesting category that I predict you will hear much more about over the next 20 years because of what's happening in the last category, *information technology*.

Amazing is the best word for what is going on in information technology. If the terms open system, relational database, object-oriented database, C.A.S.E. tools, knowledge-based systems, and fuzzy logic are not being batted around in your environment, then you'd better hop on your horse and update your information technology, as you're fixing to get left in the dust. No longer will the ability to get information limit what an organization can achieve. What will limit the organization is the ability to define what information is and to come up with para-digm-breaking (creative) ideas to develop into innovative solutions in your constantly changing business environ-ment. Tomorrow—and today to a large extent—you will win on speed, not cost.

As far as its state of development, *systems think-ing* is probably in the punch card era for those of you who labored through that phase of information technol-ogy. This area of knowledge concerns itself with large patterns, underlying assumptions, and invisible connec-tions in all kinds of systems that human being create and participate in. Several of the more prominent names associated with this research are Edward DeBono, Eli Goldratt, and Peter Senge. All of them bring their own special approaches; however, no one has pulled it all together yet. I expect you will see this knowledge base grow at a rapid pace soon.

Of course, all of these categories of knowledge are interrelated. They overlap, intertwine, and can be looked at as several three-dimensional clouds, loosely connected to one another. Today's manager must have a grip on all of the areas of knowledge. However, let me suggest that you can have yet another three-dimensional cloud that encompasses the three-dimensional management cloud. Let's call this cloud the three-dimensional leadership cloud.

Just as today's manager needs a grip on the concepts that make up three-dimensional management, today's leader had best get a grip on the concepts behind three-dimensional leadership. Just like today's political consultants are telling candidates, "It's crime, Stupid," let us tell you, "It's leadership, Stupid!" Management ability is not the major issue today. There are plenty of folks with management ability and not enough of those folks have exceptional leadership skills to capitalize on their management knowledge.

On our recommended book list, you will find *Leadership and the New Sciences* by Margaret Wheatley. Dr. Wheatley's book delivers the concepts behind three-dimensional leadership, although she doesn't call it that. She relates the sciences of Chaos Theory and Quantum Mechanics to organizations. It reads easier than it sounds.

Now is where you are going to wish we had discussed Jerry's canoe, because I am going to skip right over the concepts of chaos theory and talk some more about an organization's Strange Attractor. In chaos, the strange attractor is the force that gives overall shape or order to the chaos. You can take any system (weather, for example) that appears random, and plot it in three dimensions over a long time frame and numerous interactions, and the results will be a very well organized system that has definite and precise shape. What appears to be random and chaotic has order. The force that pulls things into shape is that strange attractor. It is like an electromagnetic field. You can't see it, but you know it's there. It's real.

Wheatley suggests that the strange attractor for organizational systems is *meaning* and *vision*. She's probably right. She talks about going into a store and being able to "feel" whether or not she is going to get good service. In our business, we talk about "the feel" of an organization and thus a sense of how productive they are.

Is there anything you can do about these issues? Most definitely! The first thing to realize is that your system is dynamic—the strength of its purpose or vision was not set in granite, once and for all time. It's subject to change. If you have a good company feel, then perhaps you need to take a second or two and ask yourself why. What can you do to strengthen and maintain this feel?

In conjunction with the Wheatley book, I suggest that you either read or reread some of the Stephen Covey books. They are not easy reading, but stay with it because he gives specifics that one can do that directly affect this strange attractor that we referred to. I think *Principle Centered Leadership* and *First Things First* are good summaries of his thinking.

For those of you who feel you are not in a leadership role, you need to kick it into this gear also. One day someone may hand you a torch and tell you to lead the way. Just holding the torch won't hack it. All the torch does is light up the target, which could be you if you don't know what to do or how to do it.

# IF YOU FIND
# A LOAD OF CAULK IN YOUR FRONT YARD,
## THEN YOU MIGHT
## BE A REDNECK

In the mid-1980s, I was plant manager of a large paint complex. "Adhesives" was one of several operating units that reported to me, and I really disliked it. (Dadburn product stuck to everything.) Service was worse than awful, and we were in one of those corporate "crises" where everyone was blaming everyone else. Fortunately, I had not been with the company that long, and I was still in my honeymoon period. Here was the situation:

There were two divisions of the company involved—the Consumer Division, which ran everything but the company stores, and the Store Division. The Store Division was complaining about poor service.

The Consumer Division was complaining about poor sales forecast.

Our filling equipment—the machine that puts the caulk in tubes—was used by the Egyptians during construction of the Pyramids and was a pain to clean.

Try going from brown to white with a product that sticks to everything. That means I planned to run brown caulk every twenty years or so.

The person I was answerable to, the vice president of manufacturing, was a tyrant. I was being held to a batch-per-week goal. He really didn't care what color the batches were. He just wanted batches.

If I missed my goal, I would be publicly hanged in downtown Baltimore. If I met the goal, I got to keep my job for another week and was able to see my family for a half day on Sundays.

Within the Consumer Division there were three groups involved: Manufacturing, which had promised so many batches per week; Operations Planning, which was responsible for service level; and Transportation, which "owned" the warehouses, the trucks, and the inventory.

Someone had told our President that inventory was evil, so Transportation certainly didn't want any more evil than necessary.

Given the above situation, what do you think happened? Well, I made white caulk until the cows came home. Throughout history this amount of white caulk has not been consumed, so nobody planned to actually use all this stuff. The transportation group refused to take the product, as no one was buying this amount, and they didn't want all that evil. Boxes of white caulk were piled everywhere. I would call Cleveland headquarters several times a week asking for permission to ship the product. This was becoming like an Alfred Hitchcock horror movie. There was caulk everywhere—in aisles, lunchrooms, drawers. We considered sending the mayor some. It was a mess.

Finally after weeks of my employees threatening to have me hanged in downtown Baltimore because everywhere they turned they were getting stuck, I called Cleveland with an ultimatum. It was a conference call with the head of operations planning and his team.

"Gentleman," I said, "here is what we are going to do. At four o'clock this afternoon I'm going to ship all of this caulk somewhere. If you would like input as to where it goes, I suggest you give me a buzz. Otherwise, it is all going to Cleveland and will just drive around up there until ya'll decide what you want to do or until your river catches on fire . . . again." Those of us who didn't work in Cleveland used to harass the corporate weenies who did, although secretly we all sort of liked the joint. If the sun would shine more than two hours a year, it would be a neat place to have a corporate headquarters.

Most of the crew in corporate operations planning were natives of Cleveland. When folks from Cleveland get excited, they talk loud and fast and wave their hands. That's why you always want to give someone from Cleveland bad news over the phone. They will be talking loud and fast, but you won't hear them. They will either be waving the phone away from their mouth or they will knock themselves unconscious with the receiver. Either way you win. However, this time I miscalculated as they had a speaker phone. I could almost hear their arms wav-

**73**

ing.

"What! You can't do that," they said, and many other things I cannot repeat in a PG 13-rated book.

"Amigos," I said, "don't test me on this. I plan to *stick* to my word . . . no pun intended."

I could hear them thinking aloud, *That little redneck is crazy. I think he'll actually do this.*

They were aware of a famous saying by a great American, "If you've ever mowed your grass and found a trailer load of white caulk in the front yard, then . . . you just might be a redneck." They were terrified because they knew I had found several loads when I mowed my lawn. By four o'clock we received specific shipping instructions. Service level eventually improved; we started manufacturing what the market wanted (novel approach); and we all moved on to the next crisis.

If you were appointed internal supply chain guru for this company, where would you begin? Do you think a software package that has a fancy name like "Enterprise Systems" is going to do the job?

A supply chain is nothing more than a system, and systems are alive, dynamic, and are held together by something—just like systems in nature—to the best of our current understanding that something consists of *purpose, information,* and *relationships.* Of course, they are all interrelated. Let's look at our paint company pals from the perspective of purpose.

The natural supply chain system, although it existed, did not even look upon itself as a system with a common purpose. Do you see how this can cause some conflicting measures?

My purpose was to keep from getting hung, and the measurement system to avoid this was "batches per week." This measure immediately eliminated compliance with obvious communist plots such as the use of brown caulk. Whoever heard of such a thing? Why would any idiot want to buy brown caulk? Besides, I thought the reason we made brown paint was to satisfy those few people on the planet that wanted to turn white caulk brown.

So . . .

*Action Step #1:* Produce plenty of batches of easy-to-make white caulk. Do not stop for anything, especially brown caulk that only communists want and costs us six batches of white caulk.

*Results of Action Step #1:* John kept his head out of the noose on a weekly basis, and we began to cover the globe in white caulk.

The Transportation Department also wanted to avoid the noose. Actually the company (and I'm not kidding here) used the term "shot" to mean being fired. Transportation kept from getting shot by making sure they did not have too much inventory.

So . . .

*Action Step #2:* Do not take shipments of anything unless it's already on back order (small exaggeration), and since we already have plenty of white caulk, be sure not to take any shipments of white caulk.

**75**

*Results of Action Step #2:* Company stores continued to be out of brown caulk forcing communist home-
builders to the competition where they have the nerve
to purchase products other than brown caulk. The company alerted the CIA, as there were many more communists than we originally thought. The inventory evil
in the form of pallets upon pallets of white caulk (that
can only be stacked two high, by the way) continued to
digest the small amount of manufacturing space in John's
tiny adhesive operation, forcing pallets into the nice paint
plant part of the facility. This sent the cost accountant,
who was in charge of allocating overhead based on use of
space, into a coma.

The operations planning guys had no reason to
worry about being shot, but they worried anyway. Folks
at the company headquarters were like cats, in they had
at least nine lives. After about the third life, they learned
some neat tricks of survival, plus they were on a first-
name basis with the hangmen. One trick was to make sure
sales remained responsible for the sales forecast, enhanc-
ing the probability that the forecasts would be totally
inaccurate. That way when service level stinks they can
always say, "Well, I made exactly what you said to make!"
In the unlikely event they were made responsible for the
sales forecast, they can always say to management when
service stinks, "If we had the XYZ super-duper MRP
II total enterprise system with interlocking brakes and
up-to-the-second updates on what Sally Jones is doing
on the shop floor in Oakland, then and only then will

we have a chance of having service that doesn't stink. Besides all of the companies on the planet are going to this new software." This is certain safety. Upper management doesn't realize that you can get better results with a pocket calculator and a No. 2 pencil. Even if the company does have the 60 bazillion bucks it takes to buy this software, it will not be installed until their grandchildren are drawing social security.

The sales folks were measured on sales volume. If sales volume was below expectations, they expected to be shot. If the numbers were not there, it didn't matter why. They were in the business of applying enough pressure to someone to get the product to the store. It didn't matter to them whether Transportation had evil in the warehouse. In fact, they would like to have plenty of evil, as they perceived that lots of evil meant no back orders or missed sales. Their perception was probably wrong, but nevertheless, it was their perception and affected the "relationship" part of the equation.

What a mess! Only by breaking the rules and jeopardizing personal numbers would the global system achieve results in alignment with generally accepted business objectives.

By now, you are probably thinking, *Those poor fools are hopelessly lost and will never make a penny!* Let me tell you, they are one of the most successful companies in the Fortune 500. If you had purchased their stock in the mid-'70s and held onto it, you would be quite wealthy. As bad as the above situation sounds, when you write it

**77**

down, I have found it to be not an unusual state of affairs. What do you think? Have you run across similar situations?

So what's the answer? What are you going to do to make an impact? Logistically, the issues of a supply chain are not all that complex. In fact, why would they be any more complex than a production cell, a plant, or a series of plants? You just draw your system box bigger. One important key is to do a good job of defining "the supply chain system" or what we like to call a value added lane. But once the lanes are defined, the principles of demand flow management would apply. Flow of stuff through systems and getting the most out of those systems involves an understanding of the dynamic relationship between buffers and the ratios of protective to productive capacity of the system. The trick is properly defining the system that adds real value. This would be a vertical cut through the organization rather than a horizontal cut, and there may be several supply chains running through one physical facility.

However, policies and measures seem to be more horizontal (manufacturing, sales, divisions, etc.) than vertical or in alignment with true value added. Down the road, organizations may want to organize around value added lanes. The chain's productivity, the chain's return on net assets, the chain's service level and utilization of the supply chain system's constraint or control point might be common measures that all are held accountable for regardless of location or department. Complex systems perform much better and are more vibrant and robust if we give them just enough order (rules and policies) to maintain acceptable pattern. That means the fewer rules and policies the better.

In our adhesive example, what if all of us had been accountable for throughput and return on net assets of the adhesive supply chain? What if the bosses had asked questions of all of us that pertained to those two measures and held us all responsible for increasing them? What if we were more accountable to the system than to our individual bosses? Do you think that would have made a difference? More difference than a computer system? You bet! However, the price you pay is not so much in dollars. It is in breaking those old comfortable habits and the way we've always been organized and managed. Let's don't pave our current cow paths. Let's redo the business system; then subordinate the information system to those decisions.

# NEVER TAKE A SHOWER
# IN A HAZARDOUS
## WASTE DUMP

Our family owns some property in Cottondale,
Alabama, where Linda and I occasionally go to relax.
When in Cottondale, our dog Henry and I like to go
outside and do guy stuff, like digging holes, hauling off
brush, looking at cows, and trying to get tractors started.
When you do these types of things in central Alabama
during August, you have a tendency to sweat. That's why
Linda always says, "Don't take Henry outside because he
will stink." Henry and I always disobey such orders. It's
sort of like leaving the toilet seat up at least once per
month as a small act of defiance.

We visited Cottondale often when our daughter, Leigh, was a student at the University of Alabama.
During one of those trips, Henry and I were coming in
from the wilderness one day, and even I noticed that he
smelled like a goat. However, he had the audacity to move
upwind of *me*. When a dog that dines on cat poop thinks
you smell bad, it is definitely time to take a shower.

I was looking forward to a nice relaxing shower. I'm sort of simple. All I need is a bar of soap, a rag and some shampoo. I turned the water on and looked for the bar of soap. There was none, but there was a whole lot of other stuff. The shower was one of those plastic molded jobs with more shelving space than a small Wal-Mart. Every shelf was full, but nothing resembled a bar of soap or shampoo.

Then fear struck me. I was probably taking a shower in the middle of a hazardous waste dump. Remember, I'm a chemical engineer and I know this kind of stuff. I was in a modern-day valley of the drums. Instead of 55-gallon drums, these folks have packaged all of these dangerous chemicals in 16 cute, little bottles with foreign sounding names. I immediately rushed outside and washed myself off with the hose pipe used to water the cow. This was not a pretty sight for the cow, and she stampeded (not good for my ego).

Little did I know that our daughter, Leigh, had rearranged the shower during the summer. I had often wondered why she was always in such a rush and gave the impression of being out of control. I now know. She must spend eight out of every twenty-four hours in the shower using all of those chemicals. If you figure ten hours of sleep, she must cram an entire day into six hours. If a normal day would naturally consume six or more hours, this kid is stressed before anything goes wrong. Throw in the occasional Murphy event, and you have a continuous state of emergency.

Of course, this only happens with college students and teenagers. We would never let this sort of thing happen in business, because then we would not be able to fill all our orders. We would be working lots of overtime, our bottlenecks would give the appearance of wandering all through our organizations, and we would not be spending enough time with our customers. That is why smart business folks like us take all of the proper actions to ensure adequate protective capacity—that bit of wiggle room you always need because the best laid plans so often go astray. How do I know this? Because I ask. Whenever I ask, I always get the reply, "Who me? I have plenty of protective capacity. I would not be caught dead without it."

Ha. Do you believe that? I didn't, so I went out on a brief, fact-finding mission to determine if some of my friends had adequate protective capacity. Of course, the most efficient way to do this is to check out their bathtubs. If they have 16 or more bottles of hazardous waste in their shower, it is a sure bet they are totally out of control, just waiting for that one large Murphy event to whop 'em.

My first stop was a chemical plant where the manager was a man, which I'll call Julius so as not to embarrass him. I was struggling with how I was going to get a peek at Julius's bathtub, when we were interrupted by a phone call. It was his mobile phone carrier wanting to renew his personal contract for the next year.

"Oh, $12 billion dollars?" I heard Julius say. "That sounds reasonable."

"Twelve billion dollars for one year of mobile phone use," I said. "That's one billion dollars per month. You either have a teenage daughter, or you have you lost your pea-picking mind. How in the world can you consume that much air time?"

"It's our voice message system," he admitted. "I use all of this air time listening to my voice mail."

"Holy mackerel! When do you have time to do this?" I asked.

"On the way back and forth to work," he said. "Since we moved to Cleveland, I have just enough time to listen to all of my messages."

"But your plant is located in Nashville!" I protested.

Julius just shrugged his shoulders. Then told me about his e-mail system, his regular mail system, his management conference calls, and his staff meetings. He intends to begin answering his mail during a one-year sabbatical, which is planned for 2030. I figured that Julius did not have a lot of capacity left for stuff like talking to employees, planning, seeing customers, and taking showers. I marked him down as not having adequate capacity and as someone Henry should stay upwind of.

"Well, Julius, at least I do not have to go to Cleveland and inspect your bathtub," I said as I packed up to leave. "If you ever feel yourself getting stressed out, come visit us in Cottondale. I'll leave you voice mail."

My next stop was to visit my friend, Oscar, who runs an apparel company out west. Many folks east of the Mississippi think some of those who live west of the Mississippi tend to be a bit on the weird side and are most definitely laid back and relaxed. I was confident I would find some protective capacity where the buffalo roam. As we walked through the plant, I asked Oscar how things were going.

"Worse than awful," was the reply. "We are behind on everything. In fact, we are so far behind, we think we are ahead. That means we've been lapped."

"Oh," I said, more than a little surprised. Just when I was about to tell Oscar that I was checking to see if he had adequate protective capacity, I spotted two fellows pulling partially-completed product off the production line.

"What are those guys doing?" I asked.

"They're pulling partially completed product off the line," he answered.

"Why in the world would they want to do that?"

"So they can put more on," he said.

"Makes perfect sense to me," I said, not wanting to let on that I thought this act made about as much sense as taking a shower in a hazardous waste dump.

"Nice view of the mountains," I said, trying to change the subject.

"Oh, that's not the mountains; that's our work-in-process inventory."

"What!" I put my glasses on to ensure Oscar was not yanking my chain. He had piles of stuff everywhere.

"You have either lost your pea-picking mind or you have an MRP II system that is run by your teenage daughter," I told him. "Why would you even consider having such a mess?"

"Oh, we're just pulling a little ahead to keep the cutting department busy. We can't afford to have that machine down."

I picked up one of the bundles. "Holy mackerel! This thing isn't due until November 4."

"But it's only October 28 now," Oscar protested.

"You're correct—October 28, 1995. That order is due November 4, 1998. You have three years of work-in-process inventory. People might not be wearing clothes in three years. All of this junk is liable to be obsolete. At least I do not have to inspect your bathtub."

Oscar was using capacity to produce things that he did not need, and then was concerned because he did not have remaining capacity to produce things that he did need. This is not an uncommon problem.

Do Leigh, Julius, and Oscar operate systems that are likely to maintain short-term stability, or are they stressed and running on the edge? Running on the edge is risky because the system can quickly move into a turbulent transition state, which may adversely affect stability.

What's a turbulent transition state? To take an everyday example, let's say you're driving down the road at 55 miles per hour. There's a sudden downpour, which darkens the sky and dramatically reduces visibility. You switch on your windshield wipers and headlights, but you maintain your speed, even though the road conditions have changed considerably. The road becomes slick and you're hydroplaning, but still you're in a hurry to get where you're going. At this point, you are in a transition state. With luck, you'll get to your destination in one piece. But a gust of wind or a slight miscalculation of the driver of the car in front of you or one of a dozen minor occurrences could have you and your car wrapped around a telephone pole in two minutes. It could go either way. By careening forward under dangerous conditions, you are definitely running on the edge and thumbing your nose at stability.

I am not advocating stability, as things are going to change anyway, but I am advocating that perhaps you should have some input into your transition. If you run your system on the edge, with no protective capacity, you radically lessen your ability to have a positive impact on your organization's destiny.

How do you know if you have a problem? First, go check your shower, and if all is okay, stroll through your business and ask these questions:

Are you working lots of overtime?

Does your constraint or bottleneck wander around through the system?

Do you have finished goods inventory at the same time you are having trouble meeting due dates?

**87**

Are folks fussing at you more than normal?

Do you have lots of inventory or work-in-process lying around?

Do you still have to expedite a bunch?

Is your sales force in a foul mood?

If you answer yes to several of these questions, there is a chance that you might be approaching a problem. What should you do? You can either truly change your system or add capacity for some temporary relief. For some, we believe this is a critical issue. Many firms, under the umbrella of "right-sizing, down-sizing, or capsizing" are not changing their business system flow; rather, they are just chopping heads and expecting the remaining people to pick up the slack. They've eliminated all of their protective capacity. Folks, this is not going to work. There will be major pain to bear down the road if this trend is not reversed. Extra capacity isn't excess capacity. It's that protection you need against all the things that can possibly go wrong.

# LOOK! UP IN THE SKY!
# IT'S PROTECTIVE CAPACITY!

The concept of protective capacity has been tough to communicate. A lot of people either refuse to get it or else they understand but do not align their actions with their knowledge. It's like smoking—even though we understand we shouldn't smoke, a lot of people do it.

So I'm going to take another shot at protective capacity, using a true story that all you high flyers should be able to relate to. Several weeks ago I had an unusual experience. I flew to Raleigh, North Carolina, and my departing flight left and arrived on time. And get this—so did my return flight. Amazing! I believe this is the first time it has happened this year, and I fly a lot.

I usually fly US Airways, but this time I had switched to Southwest. Southwest was less than half the price (I'm cheap), they have a great reputation for being on time, and they fly a real jet (US Airways has commuter service).

I am a longtime flyer on US Airways, going back to when they took over Piedmont Airlines. I was concerned that service would decline when US Airways took over Piedmont , but I was pleasantly surprised. It has

**89**

been a ten-year roller coaster ride with respect to service on US Airways, but for the most part, service has been good to excellent. I also have a bazillion miles with them. At one time, they treated you special if you had a bazillion miles, and we all like to be treated special.

In addition to being cheap, I am also a creature of habit. Sometimes my creature-of-habit side overrides my cheap side, and I would fly US Airways even though another airline might cost less and have a direct flight. This loyalty to US Airways was so strong that I have been in a state of denial with all of their problems recently. Here are a few quick incidents:

Missed getting to a client site for the first time in 11 years, as a consultant, because of a carrier. No bad weather—just 14 hours of ineptitude that included sitting on the tarmac for three hours prior to canceling all flights to my destination. Again, no weather problems. Fortunately, one of our other consultants was able to get there and the customer was not affected.

Lost luggage, for the first time ever. And the luggage is still lost although it has a name tag on it nearly the size of the bag itself that has address, phone number, and so forth. This was on a direct international flight.

Having to assume the crash position because there was an indication that the landing gear was not down. Fortunately, it was.

Canceled and delayed flights becoming the norm rather than the exception. This results in getting to hotels late and loss of sleep. When you get old and cantankerous, that's an issue. The upside is you get a lot of exercise running from terminal to terminal.

Delayed exiting a plane because they couldn't figure how to get the door open on one of the new Airbuses.

Delayed in exiting planes because of another plane at the gate, no one to guide the plane into the gate, the person operating the gate did not know how to line it up with the door, and no one to operate the gate.

A flight canceled because they were short one flight attendant. They flew a perfectly good airplane back to the place everyone wanted to go, leaving an entire planeload of people to fend for themselves.

A couple of bounced landings that would have embarrassed Captain Kangaroo.

Because of what we do at Chesapeake, I am always looking at stuff from a total systems perspective. It is a curse. When I begin to see the erosion of protective capacity, I can easily forecast a loss of predictability, a decrease in throughput velocity, and a general sense of disarray. Stick with me here. This will make perfect sense in just a minute.

There are other symptoms at US Airways such as:

Disgruntled employees. Many wear yellow ribbons indicating they are unhappy. Also their mechanics are threatening to strike.

Long lines and lots of work-in-process—in the form of all us passengers standing around.

More mistakes and shorter tempers.

So what happened to US Airways? What did they do to transform themselves from a good supplier to one that is bad? Why is Southwest so much better? In my book, faster, cheaper, more predictable, and superior service translates to better.

Let's briefly compare the two from the perspective of their transformation process and protective capacity.

Southwest seems to have a superior transformation process. Some notable differences:

Southwest has only one model of airplane. They fly a Boeing 737. This yields one type of pilot, one type of mechanic, and common spare parts. Since maintenance and flying the aircraft are pretty key items in their transformation process, this is a huge advantage.

A simplified boarding process. Normally a Southwest plane is at the gate only 15–20 minutes. From wheels down to wheels back up again, it is about 30 minutes.

That's significantly different from what US Airways has to work with.

However, the transformation system you currently have is the one you currently have. (How about that for a brilliant statement?) In the short run, US Airways is stuck with its current transformation process. The Chairman of US Airways is not going to walk out of his office, snap his fingers, and magically bring into being a new process. When you're stuck with a less than ideal transformation process, you have to make the best of it.

One way to do that is to have adequate protective capacity to ensure the stability that makes for the level of predictability and speed that your market requires. That is a real important sentence. A lot of folks don't understand that, and consequently, their results suffer.

Let me interrupt our train of thought for an important injection—I am not saying, "Do not change your system." In fact, I am a huge advocate of changing the system. However, depending upon your industry, this sort of change can take several years. Creditors, bankers, stockholders, and other stakeholders are not going to wait that long. You need to figure how you are going to get results now.

Let's compare Southwest and US Airways on levels of protective capacity. Southwest seems to have enough employees to comfortably get the job done. Again, this is relative to the transformation process that they have. Their process inherently takes fewer people to run in a stable manner. So although they looked relaxed and there is some idle time, they are getting a lot done. More importantly, they have the catch-up ability to respond when variation hits. Even with their superior system, they would be in trouble if they trimmed capacity.

Recently, US Airways seems to have just barely enough capacity, and it looks like they are trying to balance capacity to market demand. They have trimmed back maintenance resources and other areas. At the same time, they changed to a new computer system—which takes additional resources in the short run—and are adding yet another model of aircraft to their fleet. All this adds up to more complexity, an increased chance of variation, and therefore, *more* need for protective capacity. Since they have *less* capacity than before, this causes instability and thus a lack of predictability and velocity.

This translates to degradation in business results. On January 8, 1999, their stock was selling for $62.25 a share, and on September 15, 1999, it was selling for $25.44. In a letter to stockholders and analysts they wrote, "This poor operational performance is creating passenger dissatisfaction, which, we believe, is impacting our ability to generate revenue." No poop there, Sherlock Holmes. I hope they are not paying that business Einstein a lot of money.

Remember, until recently US Airways was satisfying the majority of its customers, even with its inferior transformation process. The only thing that has changed is a reduction in protective capacity under the cloak of cost reduction. I think this happened when Stephen Wolf, who is a visionary leader, handed over much of the running of the company to his second in command, who evidently is more of a manager. Putting "managers" into leadership positions can yield some predicted results. Managers are more obsessed with "efficiency" and do not have a broader, more global perspective. They will tend to look at the efficiency of a local operation in isolation. Do this throughout a complex system, and you end up making decisions that strip the organism of protective capacity, making it slower and less predictable. That translates to poorer business results, which US Airways is experiencing.

I think US Airways is an excellent example of what happens when a company trims capacity without first making a significant change to the transformation process. Sadly, they are not alone.

Companies are not the only ones guilty of consuming all protective capacity. I see the same thing happening with individual people. The inevitable destination is professional burnout, or worse yet, a nervous breakdown or similar event. As individuals, we need time to recharge and have some recreation (re-creation). Folks, your personal organizational systems also need protective capacity. Run the thing at 100 percent, and you will eventually pay the price.

What's the advice here? Learn more about the issues of protective capacity, and then align your behavior with your knowledge. We're doing it at Chesapeake Consulting. We just lengthened our vacation; we do not travel on weekends; and we have instituted a sabbatical policy.

# AND JUST
# WHAT IS
## A MURPHY MAGNET?

Helping our clients proactively address Murphy's Law is one of Chesapeake's specialties. We are no strangers to the truth that if things can go wrong, they will go wrong, and a highlight of our firm's weird culture is the annual Murphy Awards banquet. Although we ensure that our own folks are recognized, you don't have to be a Chesapeake employee to win an award. For example, last year one of our customers was recognized for locking his keys in a rental car with the engine running, blocking the exit to the world's largest monomer plant at quitting time. Oh yeah, the car was also in gear. You don't even have to be totally human. One year Lisa Scheinkopf's dog helped Lisa win an award by eating the CD-ROM drive on the company computer. This was after the dog had seen a doggie shrink for less than calm behavior.

The competition is always stiff. My daughter, Leigh, threw her name in the hat after she graduated from college and accepted a job in Dallas. Her boyfriend, Jonas, helped her move all her belongings (bless his heart or it would have been old Dad lugging the 800-pound sofa to the second-story apartment) in a packed U-Haul trailer. About nine hours after they left the resort town of Cottondale, Alabama, Linda answered the phone and it was Leigh. Linda's end of the conversation went something like this, "Oh, you only ran into a building? Thank heavens! I thought it was something serious." Linda's placid demeanor comes from being married to a Murphy Magnet for 25 years. Come to find out, Jonas, who may have some Murphy genes of his own, tried to squeeze this 11-foot high rental truck under a 10.5-foot awning, opening the top of the trailer like a can of tuna.

But when it comes to Murphy Magnets, it's hard to beat Dave Oakley. Dave joined Chesapeake in 1996. That summer we were working together in Scotland. Linda flew over and joined us for a week's vacation. While she was there, Dave, Linda, and I took our client and his wife out to dinner. The short ending to this long, funny story is that with Dave driving (who was really proud of driving on the wrong side of the road and shifting gears with his left hand) and with Linda and me riding with him (thank heavens the client and his wife were in another vehicle), the car caught on fire. After standing for several hours in the rain waiting for the Scottish police to arrive, this event looked like it may have been caused by speeding down the highway at over 70 miles per hour with the emergency brake on. Now Dave denies this, and Linda claims to have seen Dave release the break, but the Scottish police and I think that

Dave might somehow be involved.

In 1997 Dave returned to Scotland. Linda and I had the good sense to stay in Severna Park. This is Dave's own account of his trip, and I think you will like his Scottish accent.

By Dave Oakley in an e-mail to the rest of the Chesapeake gang:

Ya'll,
Even though I have the utmost fear and respect for ol' Murphy, I sure dodged him a couple of times last week. I started off by pulling in my return by one day, which is inviting Murphy to dine at the table. The client's very detail-oriented secretary, Margaret, changed my hotel reservation in Glasgow to move it up one night. She asked me if I needed directions.

Dave: "Nah, I know where the airport is. If it's still there, I'll find it." (Gender blind spot exposed)

Margaret in her nice Scottish accent: "Ye noo ti onlee tay maye twoo sheeks oov eh lamms teal ti gee ye ah mayp." Translation: "It won't take long to get a map."

Dave: "Well, okay." Thinking to myself if my flawless male guidance system breaks down I could use the map as a last resort. Heck, if the car catches on fire I could use it to try to fan the flames out.

I set off to Glasgow and find the airport flawlessly. Circle the airport twice, stop at a gas station and get directions. Pack mule it to the front desk of the Glasgow Stakis and say "reservations for Oakley."

Nice lady at reception: "Soooree, coood et bay oonder aneyther nem?"

Dave: "Hope not. But it might still be for Saturday night."

Reception: "Nooop. Neh Oookleyh fur Satoordey."

I confidently pull out my hotel voucher and hand it to her, thinking this will clear up this obvious blunder. No wonder we Americans are over here helping these folks.

Reception: "Sur dees es dee Glazgoo Steakees."

Dave: "Yes?" And I'm Dave Oakley, tired American whose biological clock is wound somewhere between Curry and Sushi time zones.

Reception: "Boot de voochere is fur dee Pourt Fourtehoos." Translation: You are at the wrong hotel, you bozo.

Dave: Looking at the voucher. "Dnope!

Dave, trying to recover: "You see I have faxed directions to the Glasgow Stakis."

Reception: "Cearteenly sur."

A nice porter standing nearby: "Um gooing to dee ayrpurt. Yeh ken fulloow maye uf ye wenna."

So as I turn to head out the door, my laptop falls out of my case and slams to the ground. Now I look real smart. They're thinking to themselves: "Aye, woot poor boogered oop ferm as im elping dem? Deh moost bay daft." As I'm back on the road to the hotel, I check the faxed directions and get a little satisfaction that the directions I didn't use WERE for the Glasgow Stakis. The moral victory is short lived as I think about the laptop. I didn't print hard copy slides to use at the client design course, and I'm flying out Monday with the LCD panel to do the course. Cold sweat shoots out of pores I didn't know I had.

I make it to the hotel and check in. Get to my room to give the laptop a test run. Visions of a laptop meltdown run through my mind. As it boots, those cute little noises it makes sound more like a litter of long-tail cats in a room full of rocking chairs. Cold sweat now freezes. The CD I had in the drive comes on and sounds even worse out of one speaker. Man, I'm thinking to myself, I'm fixing to cinch a '97 Murphy already!

I decide to drop off the rental car to cut out some morning Murphy prospects. So I take the CD player out and plug it in to charge the batteries. On the way back from Avis, I cut back through the terminal and grab dinner. I start to think about the dropped laptop charging in my room. Chuckle to myself, "What if it combusts in my room while I'm gone!"

After dinner I exit the airport to return to the hotel and fire trucks are surrounding the hotel! In the lobby there are firemen milling all over the place and some coming out of the stairwell. I ask the desk clerk to tell me it isn't Room 525. She says, "Ney, dee kook woos meykin soome haggis unt hey smooked opp deh keecheen."

Whew! I try the computer before bed and it still sounds like fingernails on a chalkboard.

I climbed into bed and said my prayers to be delivered safely out of Murphy's land. And then I dreamed incredible weird dreams. There was the one with John and Meg Wheatley sticking voodoo pins in my laptop. There was one with a kilted Ed Hill dancing with Gunner to the sound of bagpipes. Then my most perfect dream. Dan, John and I are in a rental car driving and quacking frantically in the middle of the Camden ghetto searching for the Philadelphia airport. Then there she is in her Honda Accord, the Archangel of the Anti-Murphy. She pulls up and says, "Fear not, I will guide you to the Land of Order out of Chaos." As I tried to speak, I woke.

I arrived at the airport early and debated whether to check a bag or carry both on. Instinct said carry it so you'll have more Murphy buffer at JFK to make your connection. And then the voice of George Costanza said, "Whatever makes sense; do the opposite." So I checked a bag.

Flight from Glasgow to Manchester goes well. Transfer terminals from Domestic to International. Get to the entrance of the International terminal and DNOPE! No ticket! Rifle my carry-on bag and coat approximately 60 times in five minutes. Retrace my steps through the mall four times without luck. Run back to the Domestic terminal and the gatekeeper won't let me back in. Sweating profusely through 800 calls back and forth between the gatekeeper and the bus driver, the folks on my last flight, the transfer station. . . . . No ticket! The gatekeeper then asks me if I checked a bag. BINGO! They won't leave without me! One hundred forty-nine people will want to lynch me, but I'll get home.

Informed my only option is getting a replacement ticket at the British Airways service desk located in the terminal at the exact opposite end of the world! Run as fast as I can to the BA desk. Chap there informs me that they had been paging me for the last hour and a half, in a terminal where (A) my arriving flight didn't arrive, and (B) where my departing flight doesn't depart. My sense of humor barely keeps me from asking him how I would have heard a page in a place I wasn't supposed to be. The elation of having my ticket back kicks in just as I was reaching for his tie and I take my ticket from his hand instead. Make it to the gate with time to spare. Heck, why was I worried? I was taking Murphy shots and landing on my feet the whole way. Still had the ultimate Murphy palace ahead—JFK.

From my seat in Mad Cow Class, through Customs and Immigration, through Baggage Claim and Recheck, through the terminal bus system (operated by non-English speaking New Yorkers), through changing my Continental ticket in 35 minutes! Michael Johnson couldn't do it that fast! Two hours later I was having dinner with my lovely wife.

Huh, never had a doubt!!!! Dave

**103**

My gut feeling says that justice may catch up with Dave this year. What do you think?

# ANNIVERSARY WALTZ
## AT THE MALL

I hate to shop. I dislike going to stores, and I think I might be a bit on the cheap side. (That noise you hear is the roar of agreement from my wife and daughter as they read this from our upstairs bathrooms.) I am going to describe a shopping experience that validates my attitude on roaming the malls and the need to invest more in employee selection and education.

Going to Circuit City was the result of Linda's and my marriage outlasting a Japanese-made TV set. The old TV survived teenagers, at least several hundred Naval Academy midshipmen, and numerous moves. It was shot. Way back when, Linda planned our wedding date to coincide with the after-Christmas sales, so that we would always be able to get neat stuff at good prices and live happily ever after. So we made a shopping trip to Circuit City and wrote down model numbers of TVs that we liked. I was to make the final purchase, assuring that the set would be in place by our anniversary (and in time for the Alabama-North Carolina football game).

It happened that December 28 started to develop as a dream day for folks who do not like to shop. My ideal shopping experience is to walk across the street into an empty warehouse that contains only the item I want, pick it up, pay for it quickly, and be gone. On December 28, most people are back at work after the Christmas break and not out clogging the malls. To make matters even better, we start having a snowstorm. The radio is warning us every other second, *"Do not go out unless it is absolutely necessary."*

Let me assure you, getting that TV in place for our anniversary falls into that category. As I left the office, I told our secretary, "Melody, I am off to buy a TV at Circuit City. I'll be back in a flash."

There were hardly any cars in the snow-covered parking lot. Things were going just as planned! As I walked into the store, I was pleased to see that there were at least six to ten sales clerks for every customer. This was really going to be easy pickin's. I would probably be back in the office in half a flash. I found our chosen TV and looked around for someone to take my money. No one made an attempt. Now I must admit, I am sort of a below average to average looking fellow and the room doesn't light up, and bells don't go off, when I come in. However, I am the only person within 100 miles wanting to give them nearly $2,000.

Finally, this young lady comes my way and makes eye contact. (Everyone else would breeze by looking at their feet). I thought, *This is it! I am going to get waited on.* She smiles and says, "This is not my department," and she rushes off. I am now well past two flashes, so my time estimate to Melody is shot. Several more minutes pass and finally this gentleman who looks like either a nice grandfather or a used car salesman gets within shouting distance.

*"I WANT TO BUY SOMETHING!"* I yell. This is starting to get some results. Any salesman over the age of 12 has enough experience to establish a cause-and-effect relationship between "I want to buy something" and sales commission. The gentleman's name is Stewart.

"I want that TV and that stand." I tell him.

Stewart instinctively starts to go into a sales pitch, and I interrupt. "No, no. I want that TV and that stand."

Stewart doesn't give up. "Would you like to buy our special Circuit City warranty (this is in addition to the manufacturer's warranty) for an additional $500?"

"Stewart, why would I want to do that?" I ask. "If the product is going to break, then I do not want to buy it." This appears to be a foreign concept to Stewart, so I shut up before I add more confusion to the situation.

While this conversation is going on, Stewart is bringing up on the computer all of the information that concerns the "special Circuit City Warranty." He continues, "I would be remiss in my duties if I did not offer you our warranty." Translation; "I get a huge commission if I can hoodwink you, browbeat you, or scare you into spending up to 25 percent of the purchase price of this TV on a piece of paper that is only useful if the product you are buying from me is worthless and doesn't work." Give me a break, Stewart!

**107**

I try again. "I want *THAT* TV and *THAT* stand." Translation, "Stewart, if you say one more word about this warranty, I am going to stuff this American Express card up your nose." Stewart no longer looks like a nice grandfather. He is most definitely a retired used car salesman.

As Stewart is punching in the order, I notice that he doesn't have the stand listed. "Do you have the stand listed?" I ask. Stewart seems to be struggling with the computer. I can empathize with Stewart on that one. It wasn't until last week that I found out that a "boot" was something other than a big shoe.

Beside the computer is a phone with a cord that reaches from Glen Burnie to Annapolis. The phone rings and a flustered Stewart answers it. The call is for one of the young people who buzz around Circuit City looking at the floor. This girl buzzes by me, snatches the phone from Stewart, and (I am not kidding this time) starts buzzing around me while talking on the phone. Remember the long phone cord? It is now wrapped around me to the point where I look like a mummy from AT&T. I am confident this must have been planned. While I am trying to get untangled, Stewart has more time to get his act together on the computer. Stewart finally gets the bill ready to print.

I say, "You do not have the stand on there."

"Whoops!" Stewart says. "May I have your card again?"

I check my watch. I have now been in the store trying to give them my money for over a half hour.

"This is turning out to be a bigger deal than I thought," I say to Stewart. "All we are trying to do here is take my money. This should not be that complicated."

Stewart begins to sense that my good humor is fading, and he places his hand over his nose to prevent American Express card entry. Finally, after more than 45 minutes in their store, I am ready to leave. We talk about delivery, and I give them directions from Baltimore to our house. Stewart assures me that delivery will be noooooo problem. As there are plenty of units in stock, they can deliver the product in two days.

The next day Linda calls to tell me there is a problem with delivery. It appears that it will take four days to deliver the TV and two weeks to deliver the remote, as it has to come all the way from New York City.

"Two weeks!" Linda exclaims. "It's only a three-hour drive. Even the U.S. Post Office can get stuff from there in half that time!"

Can you guess what happened next? Yep, Linda and I selected another TV (different manufacturer) from Richie's TV Store in Annapolis and canceled the order at Circuit City. The folks at Richie's delivered the product on time, hooked up the VCR , moved the old TV upstairs, and would probably have mowed the lawn had it not been covered in snow. The next time we want to spend our money on something that involves a circuit, guess who will get the nod?

**109**

What is the business point of the story? Although the large retailer had invested a lot of money in a building, a computer system, plenty of advertising, and a lot of neat merchandise, they did not invest enough in their most valuable resource—their people. The much smaller Richie's did better in this area and won the business. By the way, they hire from the same population base.

# CAN YOU SUBSTITUTE HAGGIS
## FOR COW POOP?

We were back in Scotland, and while we were resting, Matti and I solved the century-old problem of how to catch the Loch Ness Monster. Sometimes those closest to the problem overlook some obvious solutions. Our solution is to put 2,000 pounds of haggis in the loch. Ol' Nessie will eat the haggis and have so much intestinal gas that she will float to the top for a minimum of two weeks, which should be plenty of time to take pictures and interview the gal before she returns to the murky bottom.

Some of you may be wondering, *What in the heck is haggis?* I think haggis is the Scottish equivalent of cow poop and a distant cousin of scrapple and souse meat. Matti is the one who actually discovered haggis. We were at a restaurant and he said, "John, you must eat some haggis, or we will not be able to say Chesapeake has been to Scotland."

"Why don't you eat the haggis?" I protested. "What is haggis anyway, and what's it made of?"

"Never mind what's in haggis," Matti replied. "The reason I can't eat it is because I belong to a special order of the Jewish faith that strictly forbids the consumption of haggis."

That sounded a little fishy to me as I had never heard of such a Jewish sect. So I said, "How about all that other obnoxious stuff you've been eating? I'm sure God is not all that thrilled about that."

"That's different," Matti said. "Those were very small offenses. Haggis is a major crime. God would strike me with lightning if I were to taste the haggis. Since you are a Methodist, it would be safer for you to try the haggis."

So I ate some. I don't want to go into detail on the contents of haggis, but suffice it to say that one of the nicer ingredients is sheep stomach, and it goes downhill from there. Several hours later, Matti and I were taking our after-dinner walk, and it felt like the Loch Ness Monster was trying to escape from my insides. I conveyed my dismay to Matti.

"John, this is no surprise," he said. "You ate haggis! Did you read what was in that stuff?"

I survived to write this book, and Matti has been promoted to marketing director of our Baghdad office. When you see Saddam Hussein on TV discussing Theory of Constraints concepts, look for Matti in the background. He is the bald fellow with a foot in his mouth.

I later learned that I had messed up the haggis. The proper way to consume the stuff is for the chef—I use the term loosely—to bring the haggis to the table accompanied by a fellow playing the bagpipes. The piper recites a lengthy Robert Burns poem and pours Scotch whiskey all over the haggis. You then drink the remaining Scotch, and you and the haggis are ready to engage.

If you will recall, in Chapter 1 we discussed a situation where I was responsible for turning around a facility. In that chapter, we described how cow poop can be used to move behavior into closer alignment with the desired culture. If your company happens to be located in Scotland, I can state without hesitation that you could substitute haggis for cow poop as a tool for changing the culture.

We also made the analogy between organizational culture and soil. Before we can expect the seeds of a different methodology or technology to yield a crop, we must make sure the soil is fertile. The components of that soil are *R*elationships, *I*nformation, and *P*urpose (or *RIP*). I got that "RIP" term from my good friend Warren Foster, after a talk I gave for an APICS group. Warren enjoyed the talk (as a good friend, he was compelled to tell me that) and said he felt that of the three ingredients of soil, *R*elationships are the most important.

*RIP* are like ingredients of a chemical reaction. The result of the reaction is your soil or organizational culture. All the ingredients that produce the reaction are, therefore, critical. You can have a bunch of folks who are happier among themselves than pigs in slop, but if they do not have clarity of purpose or the proper information (which includes proper technology), they will be a bunch of happy failures (if there is such a thing). But Warren

**113**

was onto something.

Let's say results are poor, and you make the assumption that folks are basically good—which I think is a pretty fair assumption. That means your system is messed up. Your system is designed to give you the results you are currently getting. Want different results? Guess what . . . you must change or *RIP* your system. After we have clearly defined what we are calling a system, we must look at each component. (Read that sentence twice.)

Purpose is why the system exists. What value does it add? In many businesses one of the purposes is to generate profit and return on assets, as opposed to keeping all of the machines busy. *P*urpose must be well communicated, which means it probably needs to be kept simple.

Information, as Margaret Wheatley says, is what informs and forms us. It is our knowledge, our intuition, and our corporate memory. Management philosophies and methodologies would fall under this category. Of course, knowledge, wisdom, and caring for folks can also help clarify Purpose.

Relationships can be the toughest part of change, as change always involves a change in behavior. If the purpose goes from keeping every machine busy to making money, then relationships between different departments and those within those departments will change. In fact, a change or clarification of purpose, however slight, will probably cause a change in information and the way people relate to one another.

We get to see all kinds of soil in our job and can almost "feel" the quality of soil when we walk in through the door. Recently another consultant and I got to play in some neat dirt. The plant manager of a golf ball manufacturing plant called himself "head coach" and came to work in a pair of shorts. His office would be the envy of any 12-year-old, full of baseball bats, golf clubs, toys, and of course, piles of golf balls. Ed knocked over one of the piles and had golf balls rolling all over the poor man's office.

When Head Coach Al Scott took us through the factory, folks smiled and acted like they were happy to be there and were happy to see us. When we stopped to discuss a particular point, operators would come over and join in the conversation. We had our picture taken with the plant mascot, a very nice gopher named Romulus. Late in the afternoon, we gave Al our business cards, and the very next morning Al presented us with several dozen Wilson Ultras with the Chesapeake logo imprinted on them. Is their team successful? You bet they are! The knowledge we are transferring to them will grow fast and become deep rooted in such soil, making them even more successful. One can feel the fun.

On the other hand, we sometimes are in facilities where one can feel the distrust and fear. When we go through the factory, people look at their feet and do not make eye contact. Managers tell us what they think we want to hear, with that look in their eye, "I've outlived a thousand consultants." These poor folks are never very successful, and along with the soil, their balance sheet and P&L need lots of improvement. Needless to say, the change concepts we introduce in these companies and that kind of soil are less likely to sprout and do well.

You may ask yourself, "Why does a consulting firm that specializes in Theory of Constraints and synchronous flow concepts worry so much about soil, dirt, cow poop, and haggis?" I think the parable of the sower in the Bible is a great way to express what we do. The seeds here are what we throw out as knowledge for positive change:

In many cases the seeds fall on the path and do not take root. These are usually organizations that have far too many cost accountants in them for their own good. Now those of you who are cost accountants, don't get the hair on the back of your neck up. We like you folks, but feel deeply that there are way too many of you, and too many scorekeepers get in the way of scoring. Scorekeeping for operational decision making ain't all that tough. Most of you are nice folks and fun to be around. If you are an accountant with a good personality, consider getting a job in sales. That's where many companies need the help. Plus, you will be able to make the scoreboard light up.

In some cases, the seeds fall among weeds and are choked. Some of the weeds we run into are an efficiency mentality. (Remember—you've got to have protective capacity!) They are leaders who are timid about using cow poop and haggis to break inertia.

In some cases where there is progress, the seeds have taken root in rocky soil. If a good rain comes in, usually in the form of an executive or new honcho who blows away the torchbearers of the knowledge we have transferred, the seeds are washed away.

And there are those many happy situations where the roots of positive change have become part of the soil, and the system is healthy and prospers.

Just as the cow doesn't stay milked, the soil needs constant nurturing. Since things don't stay the same, your soil will be different today when you leave for home than it was when you got to work. Before you leave today, pick one or two folks in your organization and engage them in a conversation at a higher level of dialogue than normal. Your soil will be better as a result of your behavior. It never stops.

# DON'T LOOK NOW,
## BUT THERE'S A SNAKE
### IN THE SUPPLY CHAIN

Many years ago I arrived to work at a lower Alabama chemical plant and found one of our secretaries walloping a poor, harmless black snake about the head and shoulders with a broom.

"June, what in the world are you doing?" I asked.

"I am gonna beat this thing in the head until its body stops moving," was her reply.

By this time, the trust level between June and the snake was hitting an all time low. I rescued the poor critter and took him to medical to patch him up. We named him Scar (thanks to June) and made him a home in the Japanese garden that was in the center of our office. Every day, around noon, we would take Scar a tree frog for lunch. I am not making this up. Scar was indeed living a dog's life and provided lots of hoots for us engineering types. It doesn't take much to amuse an engineer.

A short time later, we caught another snake, a spreading adder, and we thought it would be a great idea to move him in with Scar, who seemed lonely for a playmate. Now here is what appeared to be a natural partnership. But when we went out to check on Scar and his friend, we saw what looked to be a third snake with two tails and no head. Much to our horror, we realized that the spreading adder was about halfway though the process of eating poor old Scar—yuck! I was not going to intervene in rescuing Scar this time. Chemical plants were definitely not healthy for Scar.

At first glance, this appears to be a strain in the trust between Scar and his new friend. It might appear that the adder violated the snake partnership code of ethics. Even if Scar escapes this predicament, I think we are looking at an uphill struggle to salvage any type of relationship here. Why in the world would the adder do this to Scar? I think it might boil down to several reasons:

He was hungry.

He could.

According to snake law, this behavior was probably not illegal.

However, from Scar's point of view, I think we definitely have a breach of ethics.

Ethics. Now there is a word that is getting more attention lately. Margaret Wheatley defines ethics as, "The way we decide to behave once we are in a relationship." I think the key phrase here is "we decide."

"We deciding," on how we are going to behave once we are in a relationship is not a trivial undertaking. If we fail to dialogue, then we run the risk of eventually having a problem at the value/mindset level, and there will more than likely be a breach of ethics from at least one of our perspectives. We will need to deal with the trust issues, which means we have to get into one another's mindset. For example, if Scar and the adder had the forethought to do this, the discussion might have gone along the following lines:

Scar: "Well, Mr. Adder, I perceive you to be a reasonable snake, so let's sit down and discuss our new partnership. How is it that you perceive me?"

Mr. Adder might have replied: "Scar, I perceive you as lunch. My mindset is that I eat black snakes."

At that point there is a good chance that Scar may have opted out of that partnership because of a conflict in shared values and saved himself the embarrassment of being eaten head first.

I think we may be approaching an ethics crisis. As I am writing this, our nation is in the middle of this Firestone-Ford tire recall mess. I guess it remains to be seen whether or not these companies did anything illegal; however, I think it is pretty safe to say that one or both of them did not act in an ethical manner with respect to a very serious public safety issue. I am confident that one or both of these companies rationalized and justified their individual behaviors as being perfectly okay and may have had legal counsel to validate these opinions. Their corporate mindsets and values were sure not the same as parents who were transporting children in a Ford Explorer with Firestone tires.

Here's another example. I used to work for a large paint company, and we were normally the number one customer for most of our vendors. We just arbitrarily decided one time that we would not pay our bills for 60 days, although many vendors had contracts with 30-day payment stipulations. We were able to get away with it, but I consider that unethical behavior. Just like Scar's friend, the adder, we did it because:

> We were hungry.
> We figured we could because of our size.
> We rationalized that it was not illegal.
> How many vendors were going to
> haul us into court over payment
> terms?

It appears that in issues involving ethics, one of the parties has an opportunity to yield to the temptation of personal or corporate gain at the expense of others in the relationship. In the comic pages today, the characters in For Better or For Worse were in an ethical struggle. The family had purchased a bookstore from a friend. In the process of cleaning the store they found some antique dolls and discovered them to be worth $15,000. Initially they were ecstatic; however, the mother questioned whether they should share the $15,000 with their friend, the previous owner. They were struggling with the answer, when the granddad mentioned that he disliked ethical dilemmas because the easiest answer was normally the wrong one.

So we've touched on four examples:

> Scar and his buddy.
> Firestone-Ford.
> Flexing corporate muscle.
> For Better or For Worse.

Every relationship we have is an example of an ethical dilemma waiting to happen. They are all based on trust, which is based on perception, which is based on mindsets/value/beliefs.

Behavior between partners of any type must go to a higher level if we want sustainable, higher-level business results. When we are in a relationship, we make ourselves vulnerable to some extent as we begin to form a new entity. As that entity grows and develops, we can become more interdependent, thus more vulnerable. Dynamic and successful value chains involve a "letting go" of many old rules and ways of doing things. "Letting go" and "leaps of faith" require trust and a stronger sense of ethics.

I think we have some challenges ahead. Business desires the results that come from good value and supply chain management. We know these results are a function of the quality of the relationship between the business partners. However, we are also in a global economy. Values and mindsets between companies of different corporate cultures are hard enough; now we need to crank in countries of different cultures and mindsets. Go back to the Firestone-Ford mess and the way their different CEOs reacted. The CEO from Firestone, which is Japanese owned, had a totally different response than the CEO from Ford.

So what do we do?

Here are some quick thoughts:

We all need to be less tolerant of lying, cheating, and stealing. Talk to your kids and mentor young associates concerning honor and ethics. Do not let "everybody does it" pass for an acceptable standard.

Have the courage to tell your lawyer to hush. Do not hide dishonorable behavior behind a screen of legal hogwash.

Take the time to communicate with your partners about mindsets, beliefs, and values. Talk about how you feel about certain situations.

If there is a serious and unresolved conflict in values, then consider ending the relationship.

Be aware of your own gut feelings. If a situation arises in a relationship where you or your organization stands to gain at the expense of the relationship, then your gut should tell you to slow down and ponder the issue harder. You may not want to put self first.

Know that most of us do not understand organizational and human behavior very well and that we need help. Behavioral science actually is a science (and that is coming from an old chemical engineer who used to think all those folks were flakes).

# LET'S MAKE MONEY
# AND HAVE FUN

At Chesapeake, we actually eat our own cooking. So we've just completed several days of planning, using the Theory of Constraints planning stuff. The first morning several folks were late returning from our first break. I overreacted and was a bit of a "butthead" (young person colloquial term of endearment according to my daughter). I made mention of how much this meeting was costing us, how rude it was to hold up the works, etc. The atmosphere became tense, and there was an uncomfortable silence.

Then Dave "Set the rental car on fire in a foreign country while taking the customer to dinner" Oakley blurted out, "Hey, what would Quad Graphics do in a situation like this?"

The entire group of Chesafolks shouted at the top of their lungs, "DANCE!"

At the same time, Dave hit a button on his computer. Out came the Latin beat of some conga line music. Do you sense a setup here? Immediately all of these consultants, most of whom have engineering and science degrees and have held responsible direct line positions, jumped up with their hands on each other's hips, and started shaking their booties around the conference room in time with the music. Somewhere Dilbert was hiding his face in shame.

It is a good thing I am writing this newsletter and not Ed "Get in the hot tub with the customer" Hill (Ed has won our Customer Intimacy Award) or Dan "Dancing in the streets of New Orleans" Hicks. They would have a biased slant.

Ed, Dan, and I recently had the wonderful opportunity to work with the folks at Quad Graphics. The people at Quad work hard, and they play hard. Last month we helped them put on their Quad University for all of the managers in the company. Each "university" is a two-day event, and between the two days they have a party with a band and the works.

The safe way to attend one of co-founder Harry Quadracci's parties is to stay far away from the pool so you do not get tossed in. Ed and Dan were safely away from the pool, but I was willing to take a risk and was closer to the action in order to have a business discussion with one of the managers. Again, it's a good thing that Ed and Dan are not writing this as there would be a distorted account of the facts. All of a sudden, one of these spontaneous conga lines got cranked up, and being too close to the action, I got sucked into the vortex of this thing as it breezed by me. I found myself with hands on the hips of the person in front of me, hopping around this swimming pool in the middle of Wisconsin. This was definitely a breach of the redneck code of ethics and somewhat out of character for me. And it was not a pretty sight, as I'm just about the last person on the planet that you can imagine hopping around in a conga line.

Guess what? Neither Ed nor Dan said anything, so I thought to myself, *I made a total fool of myself, and the only folks here who know me were asleep at the wheel and didn't see it. Yes!* Little did I know that Ed and Dan were taking copious notes, e-mailing all their friends and relatives, and figuring how to best use this information. The first sign of their work was at the above meeting.

Some business people would have had an instant heart attack as they calculated how much all this fun cost. Over 1,000 people went through these two-day events in four separate sessions, each one held at a nice conference center. After spending all this money on fun and education, do you think Quad Graphics is successful? If you use as your gauge "To make money in order to increase shareholder wealth and to have fun," then they are very successful. They have built over a $1 billion business in less than 30 years. They are employee-owned, and many of those employees will retire as millionaires, and they certainly have fun.

Although we preach it all the time, Harry is one of the few business folks I know who grasps the concept *"It is necessary to have capacity to consume opportunity."* He actually builds plants before he has the orders to justify adding capacity. This way of operating flies in the face of conventional wisdom about driving down operating expenses. This way of doing business means that you

**129**

strive to always have a bit of extra capacity, instead of being pared to the bone. It means that when a great idea or opportunity comes along, you're ready to capitalize on it.

Let's look at this capacity question from the customer's point of view. Have you ever arrived at the airport to find that your flight has been overbooked, and you've been bumped? How did you feel about that? Or you've only got a few minutes to eat lunch so you head for the local "fast-food" eatery. Twenty minutes later you're still standing in line, with a dozen people ahead of you. Or you've responded to a church's marketing messages and showed up for Sunday service, only to find there is no place to park. It's safe to say that your feelings about that airline, that restaurant, and that church are negative. It's even fairly likely that you'll decide never to darken their doors again. They've promised what they could not deliver, and the market is unforgiving about empty promises.

If you as the producer outsell your capacity, the market will cut you down to size. It's self-correcting. You must make the strategic decision either to lead with capacity or lead with demand, and by capacity I don't mean just plants and machines. People, their knowledge, and their commitments constitute enormous and vital capacity of any human system.

If we embrace the concept that people are our most valuable asset in an enterprise, then perhaps we should spend more time having fun and educating for the sake of educating. Harry and Betty Quadracci, husband and wife co-founders of Quad Graphics, feel that it is not the large that eat the small, but the fast that eat the slow. The smarter and happier you are, the faster you get. Whatever they are doing has certainly worked for them.

Crown Manufacturing in New Bremen, Ohio, a manufacturer of high-quality electric lift trucks, is another extremely successful company that has fun and places a high value on education. Their high-tech training facility puts many of the Fortune 500 folks to shame. Although they wear ties to work and frown on conga dancing in the conference room, there is always laughter, plenty of joking, beautiful facilities for work, and lots of smiles. Are they successful? You bet. The Dickie family has plants all over the world. Sales have doubled over the last decade, and they have begun their fourth successful transition of family leadership.

Lisa "Her dog really ate the CD ROM drive after it completed dog shrink school" Scheinkopf used to work for W.L. Gore and Associates, maker of Gore-Tex™, where the company motto was "to make money and have fun." The company even limited the size of plants to increase the odds of good, interpersonal relationships.

Bethlehem Steel's Sparrows Point Division has a very successful Theory of Constraints implementation. In addition to software, they invested as much time and effort in education as any company I have seen. Does this large steel maker also have fun? You bet! During one of our education sessions, one of the students (who was also a waterman) brought in some Maryland blue crabs and taught the rest of us the fastest way to "pick 'em." They also seemed to gain great joy from picking on each another, which is always a good sign. Other firms that made the same software investment and only some investment in the people side only achieved a fraction of the success as the Sparrows Point gang.

Just like preventive and predictive maintenance programs, it is difficult to calculate the economic impact of money spent to educate and have fun together, and perhaps that is why many struggle. It appears to almost be a "leap of faith" type of decision, and how do you develop business rules for that?

As we grow at Chesapeake, we are wrestling with some of the same issues. How do you know when to add capacity? How much time and money should be invested in internal training and research and development? Up until this point, it has been ol' John's intuition and a 100 percent leap of faith. What we are learning is that there are some neat forecasting and planning methods that can help give greater insight into the risk, but guess what? It still comes down to a leap of faith, the impact of which cannot be calculated until you make the jump. (And that's from a boring engineer!) So crank up the conga line music, kick up your heels, and learn something so you can do better as an organization.

# TAKE A RISK
## OR LEAVE WELL ENOUGH
### ALONE?

Have you ever had a great idea that went against the slogan "Leave well enough alone," and it did not work out so hot?

I begin my day by reading one of three daily newspapers. I normally go to the sports first and then to the comics. By that time the coffee is beginning to kick in, I can understand the headlines. Next to the comics is an article about animal and pet care. That is where my current problem started.

Some lady wrote in saying that her cat had dry skin and asked what she should do. The writer told this lady that she should make sure that her cat eats some wet food, as the oils in the wet food would help the skin. The author went on to say that this would also work for dogs. Then all of a sudden my brain went out for an early lunch, and I start thinking of what a good idea this would be for Henry, our 14-year-old dog that had been raised on dry dog food, an occasional mouse, and whatever cat food he can steal. On occasion, Henry has some dry skin.

So this idea that Henry needs some wet dog food in his diet starts spinning out of control. Take into account that Henry has done relatively well for 14 years with dry food, mice, and stolen cat food. A less creative person might be tempted to say, "Leave well enough alone," proceeding on to read Dilbert and Hagar the Horrible.

"I discovered why Henry has dry skin and itches sometimes. He needs wet dog food in his diet." After three decades of marriage, Linda is used to such revelations and goes with the flow. Later I overheard Linda telling our daughter, "Well, your dad has determined that Henry's dry skin is caused by the lack of wet dog food." The key words here are "your dad." Had this idea been something she figured was intelligent, it would have been "my husband." That evening we went to the store and picked up a can of the cheapest wet dog food on the planet. You really do not want to know the contents of this stuff. Thank heavens Henry does not read. The next day I mixed in a healthy helping of wet food with the dry food and new procedure was off and running. Nothing like the process of ongoing improvement–great skin for Henry is just a day or so away.

That night the two dogs, the cat that thinks she is a dog, and I go to bed at 11:00. The wet food had an unexpected effect. Sometime after I had gone to sleep, Henry hopped off the bed and pooped all over the bedroom—lots of liquid poop. Now that would have been bad enough. Here comes the REAL bad part. Linda came to bed much later and stepped in this mess. Worse yet, I slept through this whole awful situation—wife stepping in poop at bedtime, the major clean-up operations that followed, and what must have been a smell that peeled wallpaper off the neighbors' walls. And I slept through all this. Needless to say, Henry has had his once in a lifetime bite of wet dog food. I had the leftovers for lunch.

So what is the learning point here? The point is that Henry still has dry skin. Do you think I am crazy enough to try and solve this again? The little bedroom-pooping varmint can keep dry skin for all I care. I am still alive to tell about my one attempt to solve this problem, but I would not bet on a second try.

However, very successful companies would continue the testing, accepting mistakes as they go. Of course, none of them have ever been responsible for their spouses stepping in dog dung at 3:00 in the morning.

There are risks associated with making changes to complex systems such as dogs and businesses. We all talk about risk and the need to take them. However, do we ponder what to do when things do not work out? After a nasty, unpredicted effect, do you just pull in your horns, become conservative, and not proceed with the change? Your intuition tells you "No." However, inertia tempts us with a "Yes." Yielding to inertia will eventually be just as dangerous. You are never going to make significant improvement without some risk.

Let's continue with the Henry problem, and let's say my boss told me that I was still not off the hook, and that we need to fix this dry skin problem. Did I learn anything from the first experiment? Well, sure I did! The next time I feed Henry some wet dog food, what comes out the back end initially will not be a surprise. I will put his little fanny outside until the experiment is over and we are at some sort of equilibrium that is acceptable. Perhaps I may change the amount I give him or mix it with water as one friend suggested. This friend recently took out a life insurance policy on me.

In the book *Built to Last* successful companies were referred to as mutation machines. Some of the things they suggested are:

> Give things a quick try.
> Accept mistakes.
> Give people room and allow for
>    unplanned variations.
> Allow people to be persistent.

These traits may be some of the ones that really differentiate these highly successful companies from others. It has been my personal experience that in too many cases people abandon good ideas at the first obstacle. Kotter, in his book *Leading Change,* notes this as one of the eight reasons improvement initiatives fail. I think this is a tough issue. When should you cut your losses on something new that has the promise of breakthrough improvement? I do not know. However, I will give two personal examples, and then see if we can draw some sort of summary that makes sense.

Back in the mid-'70s I was involved in a major plant start-up. The plant produced a powder that was used in vulcanizing rubber for the tire industry. The plant was to use an unconventional approach to drying the product in order to reduce energy cost per pound. The traditional way was to take the wet cake from a centrifuge and send it through drying screws. The solvent that was to be dried from the powder was highly flammable so this was an inert environment. The "new" process was to use the world's largest continuous vertical centrifuge and drop the wet cake into the suction of a large blower. The idea was that the horsepower from the blowers would provide the energy to flash dry the product, thus saving lots of money. I was in an ideal spot to learn from this experience as I was high enough in the organization (a start up engineer) to see all the decision-making and low enough as to not get clobbered when everything came apart at the seams. The results were terrible. The process was very unstable, material would build up on the side of cyclones, and the plant would plug up. Seven stories of a constipated chemical plant with highly flammable solvents involved are worse than an un-constipated dog. A year and a half later after millions of dollars and many firings, the company threw in the towel, ripped out the drying process, and put in a lot of drying screws. This new process was not piloted prior to building a multimillion dollar plant. Hundreds of millions of dollars were lost in direct process related problems, additional capital, lost sales, and bad will to customers.

**137**

The second example came when I was with a major paint company. The traditional way to make paint is to disperse pigment in resin and solvent to form a paste and then pump this paste to a larger vessel where you add additional solvent and resin to make the final product. The initial vessel is called a "grinder," which is a tank with a big, old motor connected to a shaft and a "dispersion blade." I will not go into all of the problems this causes; however, it has worked for many, many years. In the 1980s, several firms were producing venture-type of mixers that accomplished the same thing, but gave much better product consistency. They were faster and had the possibility of eliminating a lot of material handling. One of the plants I was responsible for produced high volumes of water-based highway paint so we investigated this process. Pilot plant runs were successful, and we secured capital for a full-scale production process. There was a lot of resistance as you can imagine. There were some start-up problems but nothing that could not have been overcome with some persistence. The basic concept worked. However, this project was abandoned due to some of the initial problems. Other companies were having success operating similar systems.

So what have we concluded? Let's just throw out some thoughts.

I would be slow to abandon something that in some form is working somewhere else. I know there are indoor dogs somewhere that eat wet dog food, have nice skin, and do not poop all over the bedroom in the middle of the night where wives can step in it. I would be extra persistent if the payout were high AND working somewhere else.

Do some upfront risk analysis. What are the consequences of it not working and what are the risks? In the first chemical plant example, I think the company tried saving money upfront (no pilot plant) and was in a hurry to bring on new capacity. The risk of failure was huge.

So what is it we should learn from this chapter?

It appears to be more common than not to abandon new initiatives at early stages of failure.

This abandonment is one of the reasons why 75 percent of improvement initiatives fail.

If something is working somewhere else and there is a big payoff, be very, very persistent and make it work. A visit to where it is working can lessen resistance.

Also have the courage to pull the plug once it is obvious that a technology is flawed.

By the way—don't laugh too much about my dog poop analogy. Rohm and Haas, the multibillion-dollar chemical company, got its start by processing dog poop to produce a product for the leather tanning industry.

# We Need Discipline,
# Not Control

"Hey, Leigh, I think we have a problem with the dumpster," said one of my daughter's employees. Leigh had just graduated from college and was the manager of a restaurant in Dallas. "THERE IS A FIRE IN THE DUMPSTER—CALL THE TEXAS NATIONAL GUARD, THE FIRE DEPARTMENT, AND GOVERNOR BUSH," was her calm response after she observed the blaze. Evidently, someone had flicked a lit cigarette into the trash heap. The fire department and Texas National Guard arrived and filled the dumpster with water, and the day was saved. I think Governor Bush was out chasing Al Gore or something. "Miss Covington, be sure and remove the rag from the dumpster drain before tomorrow so you will not have a dumpster full of water when the guys come to collect the trash." Leigh made a mental note of that, and off she went to handle the other 181 crises per minute that are typical in a restaurant. Next time you are in a restaurant, just look around and soak it in. How would you like to be responsible for potential Murphy that can erupt in one of those places? Can you imagine?

**141**

Leigh could write a book that just talks about young parents with kids in restaurants. She has many "projectile vomiting" kid stories, but they are gross, so I will use a nicer one. She tells of a young father that was letting his little heathen run rampant throughout the restaurant, and he was near the kitchen. He looked at Leigh and said, "Isn't he cute?"

Leigh gave him that stone-cold stare and replied, "He's gonna look real cute when one of my servers comes blasting through those double doors with a tray full of hot food and knocks him on his butt—now make him sit down." She gets this ornery disposition from her mother.

Anyway, the next morning in Dallas Leigh was doing some paperwork and heard a terrible noise that sounded like a motor straining to do work. She looked out of her office window, and much to her horror, the garbage truck had somehow lifted the dumpster half-full of water to a location above the truck. Mental note must have been washed away by pleasant dreams. Well, everything got a bath—truck, garbage, and the poor fellow driving the truck who was not a happy camper. I asked her if she ran outside and apologized. She replied, "Dad, do I really look THAT stupid? I hid under the desk hoping he would never find me."

The comedy never ends. When she was managing a facility in Birmingham, some lady ran into the side of their restaurant and knocked off the water faucet. It was at that moment that they found out that no one knew where the cut-off valve was located. They later found that the builder had sheet rocked over the thing. Fortunately, they solved the problem before they drained the water supply of Birmingham, but it pointed out a couple of clinks in their armor of being prepared for the unexpected. I am pretty familiar with events that can reek havoc in plants and businesses, so I start rattling off a variety of possibilities, none of which she or the rest of her management team was prepared for. However, the management team was into "control," as are many organizations. I think there is a difference between control and being fit. Let's try and explore the difference.

Let's first explore control. There are varieties of personality types we all run into. (Thank heavens, as it sure would be boring if we were all alike.) We have all run across the "control freak" and the micromanager. They would be the extreme of the control issue. You know the type; they want data on everything. I recently attended a production meeting that was in a large conference room with charts all over the wall. They were measuring everything. Whenever I see a place with charts all over the wall, I can pretty much guess they are clueless to how their operation is running. The wall also looks pretty tacky; a nice mountain scene or a picture of a moose would be nicer. This particular company had numerous parts from a variety of work centers flow to an assembly operation. Their problem at this particular time was they were not shipping enough product. The meeting went on for 45 minutes discussing every minute detail of every

**143**

department. I finally could not sit still any longer and I asked, "How many units did we ship yesterday?"

Folks looked at me like I had three heads. No one answered, and there was some uneasy silence in the room. So I repeated, "Folks, don't you think that might be an important thing to know? How many units did we ship?"

Well, of the twenty or so folks in the room, nobody knew. A nice lady said, "I could go down the hall and get that information." However, she did not get up. More silence.

I finally said, "That would be nice, why don't you go get that information?" When she got back, we found that we were not doing worth a squat and did not have a prayer of catching up doing what we were currently doing, so we had some uneasy discussions on what we should and should not be looking at. The problem with overcontrol is we expend human resources looking at stuff that is not important at the expense of not looking at those things that are. A cute phrase for it is "majoring in minors." Some of you may laugh (while others are crying), but it is somewhat of a serious problem, especially in those companies that also want to reduce head count.

So how much "control" do you need? There was one description that made sense. "One needs enough order and control to maintain pattern." You want to be able to maintain a robust business pattern. That will depend on a variety of things. For example, if you are in the pharmaceutical business, you may have to maintain a higher level of control because of FDA and other requirements. If you do not maintain sufficient control products will be taken off the market, you will be penalized and eventually go bankrupt. In this example, control is a good thing. Hopefully, you get the point that we are hammering "overcontrol," not the concept of control.

Overcontrol comes at the expense of discipline, preparedness, and fitness. Why is that? Because each of those elements takes time and resources to develop and maintain. Let's take an example. Pretend we are in an environment where work center or plant efficiency is the primary driver of behavior. We collect and send up the chain of command a variety of reports and data and then routinely answer follow-up questions regarding this information. I realize this is an unrealistic example, but pamper me here. What is the impact on some of the specific issues of preparedness and fitness? How about maintenance of people and equipment? In most situations, the "run-to-destruction" method of maintenance is not the most beneficial for either machines or people. However, to do otherwise requires shutting down machines when they are not broken. Does the direct manager have incentive to take that short-term downtime? It is my experience that he will not; hence, he moves from one crisis to the next, draining human resources and ingenuity in the process. He jeopardizes the long-term health of the organization.

Fit organizations are less hectic and have much better performance. They have less self-inflicted,

unplanned events and thus better capacity to handle
unplanned events that are outside of their control (i.e.,
an economic downturn). Some characteristics and things
to look for:

- They are profitable over a long period
  of time.
- They do not overreact to
  quarterly results.
- They spend significant time on
  planning and people development.
- Although there is a calm pace, a
  lot gets done.
- They are very focused.
- They have a good sense of global
  measures throughout the organization.

So how do you know if you have a problem? I
don't know, but here are some things I would look for:

- Long and extended periods of
  overtime that exceed 15 percent.
- A culture of moving from one daily
  or weekly crisis to the next.
- Weekend work in facilities (other than
  the seven-day, 24-hours-per-day
  type found in many process plants
  and utilities).
- Excessive, unplanned breakdown

of equipment and people.
• Your trash dumpster is full of water.

So what should you do if you have these symptoms? You might need to hire Leigh to manage your day-to-day crisis until you get fit.

# CREATE A CRISIS,
# THEN GET A PHYSICAL

"Health is a state of complete physical, mental, and social well-being and not merely the absence of disease or infirmity."[1]

Once every 20 years, I get a physical whether I need one or not. I dislike going to the doctor. My vision of doctors is the witch doctor or one of those characters during the Civil War who would use a dull hacksaw on you. I have always associated doctors with pain and death, neither of which is real appealing. In addition, us "guys" think we are tough, and we can play through any problems. However, fate snookered me. I once injured my shoulder lifting weights (don't laugh). Of course, I can fix this on my own so no need to consider the drastic step of going to a doctor. I did all my normal tricks from doing nothing to standing on my head at midnight in a cemetery chanting the Navy Hymn. None of this worked, and my shoulder seemed to be hurting more.

My lovely wife, Linda, observed this for about 12 months, occasionally mentioning that perhaps I should go to the doctor. Finally I agreed to go see a doctor. Now this is going to be relatively easy—call to get a referral to see a shoulder doctor and then get shoulder fixed. No sweat! Linda offered to set this up for me. So this is going to be easier than easy. Little did I know that Linda and the nurse of our general practitioner would conspire to get me a physical exam. When I arrived, I figured I was going to pick up a piece of paper and be sent off to see the shoulder doctor. However, much to my surprise they put me on the scale, took my blood pressure, and locked me in a room with a funny-looking cot covered with paper and told me to wait on the doctor. Finally Dr. Gordon, our family GP, came in and said, "You're too fat." I think he used kinder words, but that was the gist of what he said.

I replied, "So being fat made my shoulder hurt?" I was now looking for the dull hacksaw. Before you could whistle Dixie, they drained me of blood and set up another appointment. During the next visit, Dr. Gordon came in and announced, "Your blood test confirms that you are too fat. You need to exercise more and go on a diet." If my shoulder had not hurt so bad, I would have clobbered him.

"The only folks that exercise more than me are Michael Jordan and President Bush," I protested.

"Then you need to go on a diet," he said. Since I had paid a walloping $10 for my co-payment, I figured I was entitled to more detail.

"Any bright ideas on the diet?" There are a zillion diets out there, most of which recommend the opposite thing to do. Dr. Gordon said to read *Sugar Busters* and

*Fit for Life* and come up with my own idea from there. By the way, that was pretty good advice. I am still too fat, but not as fat, and he did send me to some guy who fixed my shoulder.

My friend, Ed Ligon, was going to go technical mountain climbing (where you hang off cliffs by your fingernails) with his teenage son. I have known Ed for over 35 years, and he is a tad nuts. His lovely wife, Nancy, agrees as she said, "You are nuts! Fifty-year-old men do not climb mountains. Before you can go, you must have a physical." I wonder if wives get some sort of kickback on husband physicals? The doctor found Ed with prostate cancer. It was serious. Fortunately, they caught it in time; he has undergone treatment and is looking forward to many more years of mountain climbing. However, I hate to imagine what would have happened had not his wife insisted on him taking a physical.

We have been in business for nearly two decades. In that time, I have never had someone call and say, "Hey John, things are terrific! Our profits are soaring, return on assets are through the roof, service is 100 percent, all our projects are on time and under budget, and I am getting love letters from our stockholders and regulatory agencies. Would you come by and check us out?" I am still waiting for that call, but a couple of years ago I stopped holding my breath in anticipation. People call us when something is amiss, or they see trouble on the horizon. When we engage, we use our knowledge and skill to determine the cause of the pain and then develop a treatment plan.

We can all learn from the similarities between individuals and organizations. Just like our ability to fight unexpected disease may rest in our overall fitness and health, the ability of organizations to fight unexpected events rest in their leadership, culture, and the robustness of their business processes. Those are dynamic issues. All personal improvement initiatives that I have been associated with encourage you to focus on physical, social, mental, and spiritual wellness. Again, these speak to an individual's overall health—the same is true for our organizations.

Is it unrealistic to think we will implement positive change unless there is a crisis? If so, does that mean we, as business folks, sit around and wait for the next crisis to hit? Where is the incentive for our organizations to stay on a fitness program?

Is one function of leaders to cause crisis within their organizations in order to keep them dynamic and gaining in robustness? I don't know. I suspect that it is.

Now I am not advocating that you go storming in your place of business and break the furniture or set the lawn on fire. What I am suggesting is that you ponder some thought-provoking questions to ask in a calm and persistent manner that relate to the overall health of your organization. Do this before a real external crisis hits, and you will be better prepared to survive and thrive. Folks will respond to the "proactive crisis" you cause by your disruptive questions.

# LET'S TRY
# TO IMPROVE ETHICS

I was on a train from Anchorage to Denali when an elderly Canadian gentlemen sitting in front of me was discussing his recent trip to Cuba. He was loud talking (probably hearing related rather than being rude) and the topic piqued my interest, so I must admit to eavesdropping. The topic got around to what the Cubans thought about Americans (a term he used to describe us from the United States). This gentleman told his friend, "The Cubans do not hate the Americans. They just resent the way American businesses took advantage of them." The topic then shifted to the ethics of American business, and none of us would have liked hearing that conversation.

I started to speak up, but I had an uncommon attack of good judgment. Perhaps it was better to just sit and reflect on what he said and not react based on my own prejudices. I have been immersed in American business for over 30 years and have been a proud American for over half a century. I might have some preconceived ideas.

We recently did a poll on our web site, and of those responding, more than 40 percent felt that the ethics of their company were not in alignment with their own personal ethics. There are a lot of things wrong with polls. The answers might not be factual; however, one thing is factual—people's perceptions are real to them. Many times behavior is in alignment with perception. Communications are definitely affected by perception. So whether folks are right in their assessment—or wrong—it is still a serious issue. It affects communications.

A news program did a segment on University of Virginia students cheating in spite of the school's heralded honor code. Some of the professors and administrators were dismayed, as there did not seem to be a sense of outrage on the part of the students. It was as if everyone did it, so was it all that bad?

How do you establish companies where folks feel their ethics are in alignment with their personal ethics? I will give you my opinion, not as a consultant, but as one who also works and lives within a company. From an ethics point of view, I feel good about the company I'm with now. Let's first babble a bit about ethics, and then I will share with you some of the things I think we do right.

Have you ever heard the expression, "There is honor among thieves"? I understand that even gangster hit men have a code of ethics of where they will or will not "hit" you. Somewhere along the line, these bad guys learned what was good and bad in their world. Perceptions of how we should behave and thus what's ethical already exist. It has been my experience that most of the time those perceptions are not verbalized. The problem this creates is that one person might think they are operating in an ethical manner where the other feels there has been a breach. Here is an example:

I recently completed serving four years or so as head of our church council. During that time I engaged in a working relationship with several pastors. Some behaved in an ethical manner, and some did not. Of course, this is based on my preconceived ideas on how pastors should behave. One pastor lied about some church expenses, and as a married man, he was dating someone other than his wife. I think that might make anyone's list as a tad bit unethical. I made it a habit of having lunch with this person's replacement. In my opinion, the new minister crossed over the line several times in her assessment of the staff and members of our congregation. She said some things I felt were unkind. The problem might have been mine. I was having a hard time reconciling a spiritual leader being so political. I am sure she did not feel anything was wrong, and I did not say anything. That was my mistake. I missed an opportunity to improve a relationship (the new pastor and me) and perhaps the ethics of our church. I should have said something in a nonjudgmental way to let this minister know my perception of good and bad behavior from a spiritual leader. So I guess we were both unethical.

**155**

A breakdown in honor involves the ongoing conflict of "self" and truth and doing what is right. To lie, cheat, deceive, or steal is a misguided attempt to protect or glorify "self." A mishap in honor is the foe of what is good, and on occasion, we all fall short. Show me someone who claims otherwise, and I'll show you a liar. We need each other to stay on track.

Here are some thoughts on how to proactively create and establish an environment where anyone would be proud. I totally understand that I am on a ledge here, and this is just my opinion. I might be as messed up as Hogan's goat.

*Hire the right folks.*

How is that for judgmental? So who are "right folks?" I think they are people that on average stand for something greater than themselves. You may want to call that "purpose driven," where the purpose is something other than self-gratification. Now everyone has an ego and some level of selfishness, as that is probably the way we are created. However, some folks seem to have it more under control than others. If you hire people that are not honorable, you will not have an honorable culture. I also believe this is something you can pick up on an interview if you "listen" carefully.

Honorable folks keep honorable folks honorable. It is with some degree of regularity that one of my colleagues at Chesapeake will lift up a particular situation.

Are we doing the right thing? Is this behavior in alignment with our values, principles, and purpose? Is this in the best interest of our folks and the client?

If you are able to develop a culture of honorable servant-leadership, then the system can live through a bad hire. It might be painful, but the good culture will eject self-centeredness like a virus. Self-centeredness is the root cause for dishonesty.

*Minimize temptation by having an open system.*

The more clandestine and secretive, the more the opportunity for dishonesty. Several years ago we had a pretty intense IRS audit. That is not a pleasant experience, as when they make the decision to do the audit I believe they already think they "got you." We passed this without even a recommendation. It may seem a little warped, but I believe I am as proud of that as anything else we have done. Here was the awful IRS bound and determined to nail us, and they gave us a clean bill of health without so much as a recommendation.

Other than individual salaries, our financials are open to everyone. Profits and cash flow are right there for everyone to see and to see how they are dispersed. Our accounting method (TOC accounting) is simple to understand. I shudder at the complexity of some profit and loss statements—simple and clearly stated increases the odds of no one "cooking the books" or playing games by being deceptive via complex numbers. Many of Enron's problems were shrouded in complex accounting.

*Play, laugh, and serve together.*

We give away a tad more than 10 percent of our profits before tax and bonus to charity. It is something we love to do. As an individual, do you recall how good you feel when you do good for someone? Organizations are the same way. Serving folks makes us feel good about ourselves and is an honorable thing. In addition to giving away money, we go as a team and do work for Bello Machre, a charity that provides homes for the developmentally disadvantaged. Landscaping, painting, cleaning, and decorating for holidays are some of the work we have done together.

A friend of mine owns a company that recently had a union organizing campaign. Such a campaign is symbolic of workers saying, "I don't trust you!" I wonder if that trust would be greater if the executives and the workers sweated together doing good for someone else.

We have an annual Murphy Awards Banquet. When you have a bunch of consultants traveling all over the continent, funny things happen. We celebrate the funniest events and have highlighted some in these newsletters. We have a blast, but the Murphy banquets have a very pointed, organizational purpose. They serve to make sure we do not take ourselves too serious. We take what we do seriously, but humbling ourselves is a good thing.

*Be fair with wealth.*

I know that sounds stupid. However, many corporate executives are overcompensated relative to other stakeholders in the company, including us poor stockholders. This is obscene and not honorable. These executives take very little risk for the rewards they receive. I do not begrudge Bill Gates his billions—heck, he took the risk to go into business, and along the way, he made a bunch of folks rich. However, most executives are not the founders nor do they have a lot of their own personal money tied up in the company—they are employees. I think many of them have lost sight of that. I do not know when corporate salaries began spinning out of control; I just know they are.

So how does that affect ethics? I know it is easy and popular to pick on Enron. Does making ten to a hundred million dollars in salary, bonuses, and stock options foster an unhealthy ego and self-centeredness? I think it probably does in most cases. If it fosters self-centeredness, then it fosters dishonesty.

Talking about Chesapeake finances in a book is awkward for a variety of reasons. Although I am the founder of Chesapeake, I consider myself an employee and take salary and bonus like everyone else in the company. That is what makes me personally comfortable. Are we fair in how we disperse money? Some would probably say we are, and some would say we are not. I do think the relative compensation in our company is more in line with what is "fair" compared to companies where the compensation differential is a source of dysfunctional self-centeredness and thus, dishonesty.

*Set a good example.*

A friend of mine, John Croyle, wrote the book *Bringing Out The Winner In Your Child.* Since John and his wife, Tee, have raised two of their own children plus approximately 1,500 children on his boys and girls ranches, he figures he knows something about the topic. One story he tells in the book is about purchasing a radar detector. I am not going to imply that John might speed along the roads of northeast Alabama. He was riding along with his son, Brodie, and Brodie asked, "Dad, do we obey the law?" John affirmed that they did. Then Brodie asked, "Then why do we have this radar detector?" John backed off the gas and removed the radar detector. By the way, if you are a college football fan, you will recognize Brodie as the outstanding quarterback for the University of Alabama from 2002–2005.

If you hold a leadership position in your company, do the best you can to set a good example. Folks learn from you with their eyes, not their ears.

I think each of us could write a book on ethics as we all have a lot to say. I think one thing is true for every company. We can all strive to improve and purposely do things that create an environment in which ethical behavior will flourish.

# COMPUTER FOLKS
## ARE CRAZY

About once every five years or so, I feel it is my duty to ensure we all have not gone nuts on electronic stuff. This time period is normally brought to my attention by the electronic gods themselves, as they severely trash me for being lulled into some sort of false sense of security. The last twelve months have had four crowning events.

Event One: It happened while I was visiting our place in Alabama, and our daughter, Leigh, was there. I had been checking e-mail, and there was a phone cord running from the table where my laptop was to the phone jack on the floor. Leigh came into the room, and I made mention of the tripping hazard. Although she is a former gymnast, with the balance beam as her best event, walking across a flat surface has always been somewhat of a challenge. Well, so much for the warning. Next thing I knew, I heard an "Oh, #$%^&*!" I looked up to see my computer airborne, fixing to crash face down on the floor. The word "backup" had not been part of my vocabulary. Hard drive was squished, and it was going to take a bazillion dollars to retrieve the data.

Event Two: Proof that things really can go from bad to worse. We had been experiencing problems with our IT service provider and changed vendors. The former provider had been installing "patches" on our system, which is the equivalent of being held together with duct tape and chewing gum. All IT folks are nuts; it is just a matter of degree. The new guy, who was nuts, came in one day and said the famous last words, "I'm going to take the system down. It will only be five minutes." Well, he attempted to change some sort of password, and the duct tape and chewing gum began to unravel exponentially. You want to talk electronic nightmare? I could write an entire book on that one, but my blood pressure would go up. Suffice to say we now outsource most of this function, and the one person that does come in and help us calls himself a "geek on call."

Event Three: My Palm Pilot went totally on the fritz. I had the cheap kind where you change out the batteries every month or so. My good, old Palm Pilot must have not wanted its batteries changed, as it totally went kaput. You are probably thinking, *What about backup?* See Event One.

Event Four: My trusty cell phone . . . I had one of the really boring black types that received calls and allowed me to make calls. The thing just finally wore out, so I needed a new one. I sensed I was going to be in trouble when I saw a TV commercial that has this nice, young lady taking a picture with her cell phone while skiing and e-mailing it to her boyfriend, who was laid up on crutches back at the lodge. He probably tried to take a picture with his cell phone while snowboarding and crashed into a tree. Sure enough, I can do wonders with my new cell phone. With my new phone I can purchase stock, send text messages to India, check baseball scores, and launch a missile. However, making and receiving calls is somewhat of a challenge, but my screen is in color. And although I am not nearly as cool as the girl on skis, I am definitely cooler than the average "Joe cell phone user." I just can't communicate quite as well.

I do not want to add up how much time and money we spend on electronic stuff. However, when we did our budget this year, several of us did vote to go back to smoke signals and Morse code. Dit-dit-da-dit is starting to look good.

I am just joking about the smoke signals and Morse code. (I think.) However, we all probably need to take a deep breath occasionally and ensure that all of our electronic toys and communication devices are actually increasing productivity. We should not be employing them because the rest of the herd is employing them. So are you an effective user of technology? Before you answer that, let me tell you about the productivity of John Wesley (1703–1791). John Wesley, founder of what now is the United Methodist Church, was a pretty interesting and amazing character. Many credit him with preventing a revolution in England, as occurred in France. In his lifetime, here are some of his accomplishments:

• Traveled approximately 250,000 miles—by foot and horseback. He once said he needed to travel at least 4,500 miles per year.

• Preached about 42,000 sermons, which does not include exhortations and addresses. Most preachers do not preach 200 sermons per year. If they hit that mark, it would take them 200 years to match Wesley. His sermons were more difficult as many were outside, and he did not have amplifiers.

• He wrote and published:

  - A commentary on the Bible in four volumes.
  - A library of fifty volumes known as *A Christian Library*.
  - An abridged version of the above in 30 volumes.
  - Three-volume collection of sacred poetry.
  - Church history in four volumes.
  - Six volumes on church music.
  - Book on the Concise History of England.
  - Compendium of Natural Philosophy.
  - Compendium of Logic.
  - The complete English Dictionary.

- -Grammar textbooks for Hebrew, Greek, Latin, French, and English.
- -Many sermons, letters, controversial papers and pamphlets.

• Was the editor of Armenian Magazine.

• Read over 2,000 volumes during his lifetime.

• Visited the sick, buried the dead, baptized children, and made pastoral calls.

• Organized his followers into societies and provided leadership for their growth.

• Involved in the building of schools and churches.

I could go on, but you get the point. This fellow got a lot done. Guess what? He did not have a laptop, cell phone, pager, or Palm Pilot. He did not even have a ballpoint pen, so I imagine he had to chase down a turkey to get a writing instrument.

Do you get as much accomplished as John Wesley? Will the organization you lead match the growth and be as successful? I don't know about you, but I feel pretty darn humble when I compare my work output to that of John Wesley, whether it is volume or impact.

Technology is either going to increase your personal or corporate productivity or decrease it. I have seen it both ways. Most successful CEOs are where they are and successful because they know how to harness tools (including technology) to work for them. However, I have seen many folks below the level of CEO get wrapped around their technology axle. I am sure you know someone who has "spreadsheetitus," (a disease where even a simple question requires an Excel spreadsheet) or who has a cell phone glued to his ear.

The danger of technology is it can give you too much information making a system appear more complex than it is. Complexity eventually leads to chaos, lack of focus, stress, and poor results.

So what should you take away from this chapter? I don't know. Perhaps it is to just be aware enough to ask the question how a particular device is really helping you make progress towards your goals. Is it really worth the initial investment and time it takes to learn and use it? How is that new computer system at work going to improve net profits and return on investment? What I am learning by addressing the topic is that I am going to be a lot more intentional concerning my personal and corporate use of technology and try and avoid being part of a herd. I am also going to try and make it as simple as possible, as complexity is a bad thing and normally not necessary.

# NO WORRIES
## MATE

I recently traveled to Australia with two funny Chesapeake colleagues, Bob Elder and Rick Phelps. Bob is normally a major hoot just going to dinner; so you would think with a country full of kangaroos, crocs, 14 of the world's top 20 poisonous snakes, a local beer named XXXX, and 20 million nice people with a good sense of humor who believed something funny would happen. We had some chuckles, but nothing really worthy of a Murphy Award. However, that did not deter me from trying to write about the experience.

My thought process was to try and capture the theme and spirit of the Australian national slogan, "No worries, Mate." I just thought it was cool and bought a T-shirt with the saying. First of all, they actually say that. Here are some of the meanings for the phrase taking into consideration this is coming from an American.

"I have it under control."

As a response to an apology.

I understand.

An acknowledgement to any statement in English or perhaps any other language.

Also the word "mate" has nice connotations. However, I really could not come up with a good, clean business connection, and I was not feeling very funny.

This chapter still might be a little over the edge also, but here goes. One of the things I do in the early morning is spend some time meditating, praying, and reading the Bible. My faith is Christianity, and that is one of the things we are supposed to do (by the way, I more than compensate for this by doing lots of things wrong). Over the years I have come to believe that in addition to being God's living Word, the Bible is the best management/leadership/business book I have ever read.

The scripture for the day I was writing this was in Luke 12, and the subtitle of the reading was "Do Not Worry."[2] Now my relationship with God has always been like a father and a thickheaded son (me being the thick-headed son). I quickly calculated the probability of this particular scripture popping up precisely at the time I was trying to write on the phrase "No worries, Mate." I think my chances of winning the lottery were slightly higher, so I read on to see if I could make some sense out of this passage. Failure to do so probably meant a lighting strike to get through my thick head.

Here is a quote from Chapter 12: "Therefore I tell you, do not worry about your life, what you eat, or about your body, what you will wear. Life is more than food and the body more than clothes. Consider the ravens: they do not sow or reap, they have no storeroom or barn: yet God feeds them. And how much more valuable you are than the birds? Who of you by worrying can add a single hour to his life? Since you cannot do this very little thing, why do you worry about the rest?"[3]

As a small business owner, I have sought comfort and wisdom from this particular parable many times. Once, in the early days, we had consumed every dime we had, and I did not know where the next house payment was coming from. I know some of you have been there before. If not, suffice to say that it can be a situation that produces some stress and the opportunity to worry. Worrying about the situation would merely consume energy. At the last minute, Georgia Pacific called with a nice job that helped pay the bills. I do not know whether that was divine intervention or not. I had been spending time on the phone, sending out letters and other things one does to try and get sales. I doubt that there would have been much intervention had I been sitting around on my duff wringing my hands.

The next parable in the chapter starts out, "Be dressed ready for service and keep your lamps burning." It goes on to say that you should be prepared and ready, as you do not know when the time will come for it to matter. I think the fact these two parables follow one another and that Jesus was addressing his disciples, the leadership team, is significant, and we can learn from it.

This is addressed to leaders, and all of us assume leadership roles at home, in community, at work, and situational. There are going to be stressful situations, as I think they never end. During these times, some will worry—it is natural. However, the leader needs to leave the worrying to others and stay focused on doing the right things and working on the right relationships and processes. Leaders need to ensure they are dressed ready for service and their lamps are burning. The effects will take care of themselves.

I was a guest speaker for a Chamber of Commerce meeting for small business folks. Many of them were struggling, as it has been a relatively tough economy for small businesses. I could see and sense fear and panic in some. Of course that makes the business situation worse as their prospective customers can sense the same thing.

Here is some quick advice to our small and mid-sized business friends—keep working on your processes, your relationships, your common vision, and your values. Also take time to absorb books of wisdom and look for patterns. Try and relate your business to the patterns you see, and take appropriate action. Then relax, get something good to drink, watch the ravens, and mumble aloud, "No Worries, Mate!" I think that works for the large companies also.

# LEADERS MUST
## HONOR FOLK

We had lived in our house over 18 years, and the wooden garage doors were rotten. Our first clue that we needed to replace them came when one of the neighborhood cats wandered into the garage without us having to open the door. So Linda and I went to Home Depot to purchase new ones. The price of the doors was not too bad, but then it came time to get them installed. The cost of the doors pales in comparison to what Home Depot wanted to install the darn things. "Hey, I just want you to install a simple garage door—not put in a new driveway!" Well heck, I'm an engineer, and I am not paying some dufus head sixteen bazillion dollars to hang a couple of garage doors. "Just ship the doors, and I'll take care of the installation." I could tell Linda was proud of me. I think I heard the fellow that sold us the doors chuckle.

Okay—how many of you have actually installed a garage door? The instructions start off by telling you this is going to take between four and eight hours per door (and I've got two). They even send a videotape. The idea of using the existing rails, or even some of the existing facing, was quickly squashed. This is definitely going to

**171**

be a pain in the neck, so I called Wayne, the person we use for carpenter work. "Hey, John, I do not do garage doors, but I can give you the name of the person I use."

I called that guy, and what he wanted to do was sell me two more garage doors. When I asked him to give me a price to install the ones I had he answered, "I won't even come out to look at it for less than 16 bazillion dollars." I am certain there is some sort of collusion among all of the garage door installers in the world.

"Well, the heck with it. These doors will be here when we get back from vacation." So Linda and I left for Alabama for a few weeks, leaving the local outdoor cats free reign of our garage. By the way, these cute cats are running loose in violation of Anne Arundel County law and are a detriment to the environment as they eat birds and chipmunks. Little Fluffy does not discriminate between an endangered species and a crow. Besides, most cats are smart enough not to mess with a crow, and they disrupt the delicate balance of nature. So if you own a cat and it's not a cougar, then keep it in the house and out of our garage and away from the Peregrine Falcon and hawk food. I would rather watch the falcons and hawks than your cat.

On the drive back from vacation, I was mentally planning my next 15 weekends—putting up garage doors. When we got home, lo and behold, one of our garage doors had installed itself. I figured that either magical elves or my next-door neighbor, Dave Ford, had installed this door. As we are not pure Irish, we do not have a lot of elves running around our house, so it had to be Dave. Dave and his lovely wife, Mary, had been kind enough to watch our house, and Dave saw those doors just sitting there in the garage. One thing led to another, and he installed one and later installed the other with me providing the flunky work. We engineers are good for something. Besides, I'm a chemical engineer, and we don't do doors; we do toilets.

I do believe that is one of the nicest things that anyone has ever done for me. Again, if you have never installed a garage door, it is hard to imagine. I told Dave I was going to have to cut his grass and shovel his driveway for the next 25 years.

Okay, so this is a blatant act of someone doing something nice for someone else. We all can come up with examples, and most of us have even done nice things for other people. So how does that play out in the workplace? Well, it is a stretch, but let's see if we can blend it in.

We feel there are three roles that leaders must master:

1. The role of Honoring
2. The role of Disrupting
3. The role of Aligning

We'll hit on honoring in this chapter.

Of course, honoring means what you obviously think it means—we need to honor our commitments,

**173**

be truthful, put our egos on the shelf, and place organizational purpose out in front. However, it means much more. It means honoring yourself and others.

So how do you honor yourself? You do this by getting enough exercise and rest, eating properly, continuing to learn, nurturing our relationships with friends and family, and developing spiritually. I had a wonderful friend one time that was a Methodist minister, and we would make it a point to have lunch once per month. This fellow literally had every second scheduled with meetings, hospital visits, and a multitude of other things. Although he was quite thin, I asked him about his exercise program—no exercise. I went down my mental checklist of things he should be doing to honor himself, and he struck out on about all of them. I finally asked, "Say Harold (not his real name), what happens if someone dies? Are you going to be able to tend to their needs? Do they need to schedule dying so you can be available?" Harold was a wonderful human being, but a relatively ineffective leader with respect to moving the organization forward and growing. If you are not honoring yourself, then you lose capacity. The same thing happens when you do not proactively honor those to whom you are attached. Honoring increases capacity, information flow, and productivity.

Honoring others goes much beyond just being nice. It means respecting their uniqueness as an individual and having confidence in them. People have a tendency to act as we think they are going to act. I think it is especially neat for the leader to have a higher opinion of potential and performance than the individual and create a bridge from how they see themselves to how you see them. Honoring means not assigning blame and continuing to work to put individuals where they and the team can win big. It means letting go of control and letting them run to daylight. Honoring means thinking good thoughts about your business associates, almost to the point of being naïve. It means expecting the best from everyone and actually believing it. It is spirituality at work. I have not run into many bad folks over the years. I have run into a lot of folks that were in the wrong job or being poorly utilized or not trusted.

So are there some practical things you can do to improve your "honoring" skills? Here are a few suggestions:

1. Maintain daily practices that renew body, spirit, and mind.
2. Use some sort of goal-tracking system where you integrate personal and professional goals.
3. Actively seek feedback. (That's tough.)
4. Focus on vision/mission/purpose when making decisions.
5. Invest in a strong leadership bench. This is countercurrent to many trends of cutting cost to the bone.
6. Put the right people in the right roles.

**175**

7. Create an environment where people take responsibility for their actions and outcomes.
8. Stop managing the details—understand the details, but don't manage them. Let go of some control.
9. Meditate or pray for your direct reports, customers, vendors, and your common mission. (I'm serious.)
10. Keep your cat out of my garage.

    I bounced this chapter off my colleagues at Chesapeake before we went to print. The consensus choice to get edited was the issue surrounding cats. "Do we really want to anger every cat lover on the planet? What's the point?" So twice I started to take the cat reference out. I was just fixing to hit delete when a pair of cardinals landed on the limb right outside the kitchen window. The female was about three feet from my nose and seemed to be giving me one of those looks, *Don't you take that out of there!* So I sat on it one night. The next morning one of the most adorable, roaming cats, Jake, ran across our backyard with a critter in his mouth. I hope it is not the female cardinal. Cat reference stays in. In fact, it is probably the best honoring story of the three. Many times honoring someone or something (like the environment) requires challenging some of our previous assumptions. My neighbors who let their cats roam are wonderful people, and they absolutely do not see anything wrong with letting their cats run outside, unrestrained. The fact that they would be doing something that would harm the environment would be appalling to them. However, I also know some very nice people that use phrases and language that would hurt other people's feelings, and they honestly do not have a clue that they are doing harm. Just because they do not have a clue does not take away from the fact that they are. In order to do a better job of honoring, they will need to change their mindsets and their behaviors. This leadership stuff is darn tough.

# ARE BIRDS
## SMARTER
### THAN PEOPLE?

Every family has traditions and patterns they follow. That is probably a good thing. One of ours is each Fourth of July; Linda and I go out on the boat with our good friends, Bob and Jo Beth Ireland. We travel down Weems Creek in Annapolis, cross the Severn River, and there we drink, eat, and watch the City of Annapolis fireworks. It's a wonderful tradition, with wonderful friends. However, patterns can be disrupted.

The Irelands have a beautiful home in Annapolis. (They also own the boat.) Jo Beth is quite artistic and does a wonderful job of decorating. She normally has a nice wreath on the door. As Linda and I approached their front door, something zoomed by our heads. We nearly got clobbered by a bird that built her nest in the wreath. It was a cute bird.

Let me take a quick detour for a second. Do you realize we have a bird paranoia crisis in our county? I blame it on Alfred Hitchcock and his horror movie *The Birds.* Ask around, and I bet you have someone in your family or work place that is terrified of birds, whether it is a man-eating condor or a man-eating wren or sparrows. Jo Beth Ireland is one of those folks who is terrified of birds, man-eating or not.

After eating and drinking, watching fireworks, and climbing the nearly 2,000 steps back up to the house, Bob and I were going to do some "guy stuff" like load his power washer into our van. That task took us to a point where we would reenter the house by the door that had the bird nest decoration. As Bob started to open the door, my quick engineering logic figured that if the door opened to the inside the bird would be in the house. Well, Bob has a Ph.D. in something far more sophisticated than engineering, and if he wanted advice on how to open his door, he would ask for it. Bob quickly learned that you should listen to engineers; the bird flew out of the nest while the door was open, and now we had a man-eating bird in the house. Our first thought was to not tell Jo Beth and calmly catch the bird. When the bird flew upstairs, we figured we had best send out the alarm. "Man-eating bird in the house because Bob Ireland would not listen to his best buddy John!" Linda accompanied Jo Beth to the safety of the basement while Bob and I took on the bird.

Have you ever tried to catch a bird? More specifically, have you ever tried to catch a bird, with a towel, late at night, with the added pressure that your wife was going to have a coronary unless you got the bird out of the house? So letting the bird die of old age was not an option.

Since the bird had made the fatal mistake of flying upstairs, we figured we had her. We would simply close off every room and then search each one, and surely, we will have outfoxed this bird. After an exhausted search, we had no bird. Now there was a huge temptation to tell Jo Beth that all was well and that the bird had evaporated into thin air. The bird then reappeared in the hallway, looked at us, laughed, and flew downstairs. Imagine a house with high cathedral ceilings, beautiful paintings, etc. If you ever saw the movie "Summer Vacation," where John Candy and his pal were chasing a bat around the house, you can imagine the scene. This went on for at least half an hour. We had to take several "laugh" breaks. We both laughed so hard that tears were pouring out, and our stomachs hurt for a week afterwards. Linda and Jo Beth could only imagine what was going on when Bob and I were running around upstairs. They were consoled by the fact they did not hear anything breaking.

We never did catch the bird. The bird got tired of running us around the house, so she flew out the door. (We did have enough sense to leave the door open, figuring more birds would fly out of the house than into the house). After the crisis was over and our wives joined us upstairs, we were all enjoying another great laugh when Bob noticed what looked to be a smear on the wall. It appears the bird did take the time to have a potty break (yuck). By the way, the bird successfully raised a small family in the wreath and now has relocated.

**181**

One of the three major roles of being a leader is being disruptive (the other two being honoring and aligning). So am I suggesting you let a flock of birds loose in your business? Well, if it wasn't for Alfred Hitchcock and the smears on the wall that might not be a bad idea.

Our business organizational systems are not pushed; they are disrupted. If the leader does not disrupt from the inside, eventually external forces will disrupt, and you will have even less control than you think you have now (which is probably a lot less than you think you have).

A disruptive leader is one that encourages expressions of diverse views. If different opinions are not supported, then inferior solutions and backstabbing politics may emerge. The leader needs to surround himself with folks who express perspectives that differ and create an environment where they are not belittled. The leader needs to play the role of "devil's advocate" on occasion. Focused, uncomfortable questions are an excellent way to disrupt your system.

Sometimes you need to take action, before all the facts are in, which many in your organization may consider haphazard and disruptive. Many times taking action and experimenting are the only ways to drive knowledge acquisition and thus improvement. Disruptive leaders, many times, use a sense of urgency to push the system to a state of disequilibrium, making decisions and taking actions before certainty sets in and acts as a means of getting information.

I have tried to stress the positive type of disruption. However, this is where the need for some balance sets in. Do you like to be disrupted? Most folks do not like getting disrupted. Bob, the bird, and I had a grand time on the Fourth; our wives did not see a whole lot of humor in the situation. While you are disrupting, you must also remember your obligation to honor. Make your best effort to ensure you do not withdraw such a huge amount from someone's emotional bank account that you can't recover. Don't back off the disruptions, but be aware of what's happening.

# ALIGNMENT

Aligning includes all the activities leaders must take to get everyone pulling in the same direction. At the core of alignment is the skill of being able to tell and sell the story—in all the ways necessary to allow people to see how what they do fits in with the big picture. It is about keeping the organization focused on making the story a reality. There needs to be a mental picture in the mind of the leader before he or she begins to align. Chesapeake entered the leadership business when it became apparent that the cultures of our customers were the key factor in them getting results. In process improvement (TOC, Lean, Six Sigma, TQM, etc.), a new vision of how things flow and are transformed must replace an already existing and erroneous one. This is never a total piece of cake; however, we found marked differences in clients. In some environments, things go relatively smoothly. Years later they still have the vision (and have improved upon it) and get excellent long-term results. In other cases, it is like pulling wisdom teeth without Novocain. In some extreme situations, Chesapeake had to step in and assume much of the operational leadership issues as the company leaders were having a huge struggle with their own leadership roles and abilities.

Alignment means putting a firm stake in the ground. "Here is where we are going. Here's what the final results will look like!" There may be varieties of ways one chooses to get there, but at some point in time, an option to travel to a different stake or point has to be removed. During alignment it begins to become clear where the organization is heading, which can result in some folks opting out. That's okay, as good people have the right to disagree. Once the vision is verbalized, the role of the leader(s) is to start asking questions that are intended to ensure focused behavior that drives to the vision. This process will be both energizing and joyful for some and stressful and painful for others, to the point where some will leave. My wife, Linda, noted one time that very seldom did I fire anyone, as I was so driven on alignment to purpose that anyone not aligning his or her behavior to purpose was driven crazy and would quit.

I think the best way to explain the issue of alignment is through several examples.

Recently our church participated in "40 Days of Purpose," which is based on Rick Warren's bestseller, *The Purpose Driven Life.* The intent was, for 40 days, all 2,000 members of our church would read the same book, have the same lessons, and all be marching to the beat of the same drum. Our pastors and church leaders had a clear vision all the way down to the finest of details as to how those 40 days would progress. The 40-day program was a booming success; many lives were changed and the church was reinvigorated. The overwhelming majority of our congregation was excited before, during, and after the process. However, there were some that moaned and groaned the entire way and even refused to participate. That is going to happen, especially if you are making any sort of significant change. Our pastors and church leaders did not waver when faced with the naysayers. Had they appeased them in any way, the process would have been derailed and results not achieved.

Another and much more controversial example is what is currently happening in the Middle East. President Bush has a vision of a Middle East that is democratic and a culture where people are free from oppression. His thought is that such an environment would foster world peace and harmony verses a world obsessed with terrorism. His subordinates and allies see the same vision, and you can see action plans in alignment with that vision. Agree or not, there is not much doubt where he is headed, and if you are not onboard, you will be pushed aside. Legitimate time for dissent is prior to action being taken, but once a direction is determined, then folks need to "get with the program." Leaders need to keep them enrolled in the program. This is a continuous effort as the cow doesn't stay milked.

How do you achieve alignment? I had an old friend who said, "The best way to change the manager is to change the manager." One way to achieve alignment as a leader is to remove those folks that either can't or will not get it and start with a new crew. There is a strong

**187**

argument for that approach. God was not too thrilled with the group of managers that were posed to go into the Promised Land, so he let them wander around for about 40 years (a generation) so they could enter a new experience with a new leadership team. We have witnessed many corporate leaders over the years who tried to emulate God, but just could not wait for the 40 years to pass. If you want a fast transition, then you may want to lean toward at least some "new players" versus trying to reprogram the old players. One way to consider doing this is to reevaluate your personnel. I have seen very few bad folks; however, I have found a lot of people who are in a position that is wrong for them and wrong for their organization. Sometimes if you have some folks change seats, you can accomplish the same objective as "new players." A large part of alignment is about putting people in the right positions, clarifying roles, and equipping them to do what is needed for the common good.

We have had plenty of spirited discussions within Chesapeake concerning this issue of the best way to create alignment. I will easily sacrifice an individual ego for the good of the whole, and I will do it relatively quickly. I have been somewhat successful doing that, and many times, we hold on to what has worked for us. There is another view within Chesapeake that leans toward working with individual strengths and relationships to find or rebuild common bonds. One method is more autocratic, and the other is strength-based, where you put the right people in the right seats, let them define the vision, and then all engage in the act of aligning the organization. This latter approach requires attention to rules of engagement and often involves coaching key relationships to create a noncompromise. An agreed upon "given" with either approach is that the organization must get results.

Some people mistake alignment for a culture of head nodders and "yes folks." This is not what we are talking about. A good leader provides an opportunity for dissent and argument without fear of retribution. This creates the best possible information for decision making. However, when a decision is made then it is almost like a switch is flipped; dissent must end and unified action must begin. I guess the question is how long you wait to flip the switch. If you are dealing with an immediate crisis or emergency, you cannot wait long. If you are looking at the transformation of an entire organization, the disruption, discussion, and debate phase may last a long time. In the latter case, there may be numerous repetitions of flipping of the switch. You may be traveling down a particular path that is not working so, therefore, there needs to be pause for dissent, debate, and additional disruption so energy is not wasted. It really does depend.

So what is our advice on this issue of alignment? In all cases, it is a critical role for a leader. The specifics of how a leader plays are dependent upon a leader's natural strengths and the stage of implementation of a change initiative.

# ONE LAST LESSON
## FROM HENRY

He came bounding into our lives in March of 1988, and Linda and I were with him as our vet put him to sleep. He had lived nearly 16 years and was a family and Chesapeake icon. Old age, arthritis, and a host of other problems that go with being a 16-year-old Cairn Terrier had taken their toll, and the vet said it would be cruel to continue. Linda and I did not want to let go nor did we want to see the reality of his condition. Those of you who are animal and pet lovers understand.

Henry was the lead character in many of these chapters. Real life has patterns that are consistent and repeatable; so if we observe life around us with an inquisitive eye, we can gain enormous insights that can help us to move forward. Henry was part of my immediate world and, therefore, a constant teacher.

Every leader should have a dog. There are days when leaders are just unlovable, and our customers, colleagues, and family members do not wag their tails when they see us coming. So what can we learn from Henry's life? I don't know. Let's recap the highlights with the faith that something useful will fall out.

Cairn Terriers were bred in Scotland to hunt var-
mints, and they are feisty little critters. In fact, Henry
looked a bit like the master varmint getter "Yosemite
Sam" from the comic strips. He had a ton of energy,
loved to run, chase his ball, chase his cat, play with kids,
wander off and visit the neighbors when you were not
looking, and hang around with midshipmen from the
Naval Academy. Once when he got a confirmed mouse
kill, they made him an official Marine with a little ban-
dana and the works. When Henry was about five or six
years old, Linda asked our vet, "When is he going to slow
down a tad?" The vet laughed and said another couple of
years.

At about age eight, Henry did indeed start to lose
a step or two. It was at that time that Linda was afraid
that if something happened to Henry the cat would
grieve herself to death. The solution to that was to get
the cat a spare dog (I am not kidding here), so Griffin came bounding into the Covington house. Griffin
helped give Henry renewed gusto and kicked the energy
level up a peg or two.

We actually had a subsystem within the Covington household system. That subsystem was the animals,
and Henry was the head honcho. This was such a tight-
knit group that when we boarded them at the kennel
the cat had to stay in a large cage with her two dogs or
else she would get very sick and shut down. I think we
could have charged the kennel, because they were always
a novelty.

One day we left the house with Henry, and he never came back. Griffin and Dusty were hurt and confused, as a key relationship in their system no longer was there. For several days they just moped around the house being miserable. Gradually their energy levels cranked back up, and a new system somehow took form. It was a different system, with different roles and feel.

Now let's switch gears. We did some work with a family-owned business whose chairman retired after serving for 50 years. He did a great job and was an industry and company icon. There were strong company relationships based on kinship and many years of success. Like Henry, he was the head honcho of his system. When he retired, the rest of the system was not robust enough to continue ahead successfully. What do I mean by robust? I mean that the purpose of the system and the other relationships within that system were not strong. Yank out the head honcho, and you have trouble under those conditions.

When we celebrated 15 years of being in business, my friend and colleague, Penny Gladwell, organized our confusion for the week. She asked that all the folks at Chesapeake come armed with at least one memory that they wanted to share. All but me—my assignment was to talk about where we are going during the next 15 years. Penny expected visuals, dancing bears, and the whole works, so this was no small assignment and was going to require some thought and contemplation. During this assignment, my pal Henry was struggling by my side. When I added 15 years to my current age and then carried Henry up the stairs, it made me uncomfortable. I wonder if Henry took Dusty and Griffin aside and prepared them for a day he would not be there. I wonder if he cared how the subsystem would operate without his leadership. I wonder if the above-mentioned chairman spent time contemplating what would happen when he left—were leaders in place to take the company forward?

I think many times what keeps us from making those tough plans, especially in close-knit groups, is the strength of the very relationships that will eventually be gone. Facing reality can be one big pain. So what is a leader to do? Here are some thoughts:

- Enjoy, appreciate, and strengthen the relationships you have.

- Put the organic system you are responsible for first. Make it more dynamic with new and exciting relationships in the form of new partners, vendors, services, markets, facilities, and new internal leaders.

- Calmly and intentionally disrupt the system in a positive manner and encourage others to do the same. Well-planned and positive disruptions keep a system alive.

- Have traditions and fun that pull the system together. Let the system have fun with itself.

- At Chesapeake, we are going to get stronger and bigger to the point where when I go off one day and not come back that I won't be missed. Well, maybe someone will miss me, but the Chesapeake system will not skip a beat with respect to robustness and impact.

So did we learn anything? I did, or at least I validated some things I already knew. Major change is thrust upon us whether we like it or not. We can do two things:

1. Make our systems stronger, more diverse, and more energetic to withstand change when it comes.

2. Learn to manage transitions better. Again, this comes from strength.

I read something this week saying that all pets go to Heaven. I hope that is true. Their ability to offer unconditional love sure meets the criteria for heavenly kindness. Thank you, Henry, for the companionship and many lessons taught. And thank you for wagging your tail when you saw me coming.

# ENDNOTES

[1] The World Health Organization © (http://www.who.int).

[2] The Holy Bible, NIV, International Bible Society ©.
[3] The Holy Bible, NIV, International Bible Society ©, p.775.

To order more
copies of this book contact

TATE PUBLISHING, LLC

127 East Trade Centre Terrace
Mustang, Oklahoma 73064

(888) 361 - 9473

Tate Publishing, LLC
www.tatepublishing.com